Praise for *Making Your Crazy Work for You*

"Childhood, for most of us, was a trauma from which we may not yet have recovered nor yet understand, which these brilliant authors call 'Your Crazy.' In this scintillating book, you will find not only the source of this almost universal condition but an explanation of what it is and what you can do to move from 'crazy' to 'sanity.' We commend their compelling solution and recommend this book to everyone who may have suffered trauma or who wants to understand others who have."

Harville Hendrix, PhD, and Helen LaKelly Hunt, PhD
New York Times-bestselling authors of *Doing IMAGO Relationship Therapy in the Space-Between*

. . .

"A powerful, landmark book with a novel approach to dealing with developmental trauma and all the challenges it brings in cultivating true self-love and intimacy with another. The authors take you on an eye-opening journey where your most shameful vulnerabilities are explored and transcended in the process of 'making your crazy work for you.' A must-read!"

Diana Kirschner, PhD
author of the international bestseller *Love in 90 Days*

. . .

"A phenomenal book about how our human experience of loss and grief bonds us more than we think. The authors draw from different disciplines, illuminating how our early experiences and the hurts they have caused can lead to a fragmented sense of self. We learn how to re-integrate these pieces back into our lives with patience, love, compassion, and understanding. We do this so that we can feel whole again, and maybe only to learn that we were never actually broken in the first place. This book is a must read for those who want to live a little lighter. I know I do!"

Sue Varma, MD
board certified psychiatr
forthcoming book *Prac

• • •

"This book masterfully explains how to turn your crazy into a tool that can help enhance your personal and professional relationships. We all have some crazy in us! Why not benefit from your crazy? This book will teach you how."

Tom Shanahan
author of *Spiritual Adrenaline: A Lifestyle Plan to Nourish and Strengthen Your Recovery*

• • •

"There are a lot of books out there on 'self-love' and 'having a better relationship with yourself,' but this book stands out for its depth, intelligence, and accessibility. Based on extensive research and written by experts with significant clinical experience, it is an immensely enjoyable read and a must for anyone who feels they need a mental reset to optimize their lives. If you want to understand how your past and current habits are holding you back, and how to craft a successful life moving forward, look no further. This book is a gem and I highly recommend it."

Srini Pillay, MD
Harvard-trained psychiatrist and brain researcher, author of *Tinker Dabble Doodle Try: Unlock the Power of the Unfocused Mind*

• • •

"*Making Your Crazy Work for You* is a practical guide to help increase self-awareness and should be read by anyone interested in improving relationships in their life, at work, and at home."

Dr. Santor Nishizaki
award-winning CEO, author, and business school professor

MAKING YOUR CRAZY WORK FOR YOU

MAKING YOUR
CRAZY
WORK FOR YOU

From Trauma and Isolation to
Self-Acceptance and Love

Mark B. Borg, Jr., PhD

Grant H. Brenner, MD

Daniel Berry, RN, MHA

CRP®
CENTRAL RECOVERY PRESS
LAS VEGAS, NV

Central Recovery Press (CRP) is committed to publishing exceptional materials addressing addiction treatment, recovery, and behavioral healthcare topics.

For more information, visit www.centralrecoverypress.com.

Publisher: Central Recovery Press
3321 N. Buffalo Drive
Las Vegas, NV 89129

26 25 24 23 22 21   1 2 3 4 5

Library of Congress Cataloging-in-Publication Data

Names: Borg, Mark B., Jr., author. | Brenner, Grant H., author. | Berry, Daniel, author.
Title: Making your crazy work for you : from trauma and isolation to self-acceptance and love / Mark B. Borg, Jr., PhD, Grant H. Brenner, MD, Daniel Berry, RN, MHA.
Description: Las Vegas, NV : Central Recovery Press, [2021] | Includes bibliographical references. | Summary: "An insightful guidebook for enhancing the most vital relationship in every person's life--the one they have with themselves"-- Provided by publisher.
Identifiers: LCCN 2021004173 (print) | LCCN 2021004174 (ebook) | ISBN 9781949481532 (trade paperback) | ISBN 9781949481549 (ebook)
Subjects: LCSH: Self-acceptance. | Psychic trauma.
Classification: LCC BF575.S37 B67 2021 (print) | LCC BF575.S37 (ebook) | DDC 158.1--dc23
LC record available at https://lccn.loc.gov/2021004173
LC ebook record available at https://lccn.loc.gov/2021004174

Author photos by Brittainy Newman. Used with permission.

Cover design and interior by Sara Streifel, Think Creative Design.

MARK

To Haruna
. . . falling in love every day.

GRANT

This is dedicated to the human family, to our
potential together, with special thanks to those
closest to me in my life.

DANNY

To all of us who, somehow, sometime, have let
ourselves get talked out of the idea of love.

TABLE OF CONTENTS

Introduction   Our Crazy and How We Got There ix

Part I: Identifying Your Crazy

Chapter 1   How Self-Irrelationship Looks and Feels 3

Chapter 2   Brainlock 101: Why We Become Stuck......................27

Chapter 3   Performer and Audience.....................................37

Chapter 4   The GRAFTS Behaviors: How Childhood
Experiences Keep Us Crazy......................................51

Part II: Treating Your Crazy

Chapter 5   Compassionate Empathy...65

Chapter 6   Becoming a Good Self-Parent 81

Chapter 7   A Good Enough World: From
Self-Irrelationship to Better Relationships 93

Chapter 8   Self-Irrelationship Success and Failure 109

Part III: Bending, Blending, and Mending

Chapter 9   Self-Self Assessment: The 40-20-40..........................127

Chapter 10   Making Your Crazy Work for You:
              The DREAM Sequence 143

Chapter 11   Discovery of the Self 157

Chapter 12   Repair 167

Chapter 13   Empowerment 179

Chapter 14   Alternatives: Expanding My Choices
              about Who I Am and How I Live 187

Chapter 15   Mutuality with Myself 199

Conclusion   Letting Your Crazy Work for You 211

              Acknowledgments 215

              Notes 221

              Bibliography 229

              About the Authors 237

Our Crazy and How We Got There

An old joke says, "You don't have to be crazy to work here, but it helps." All of us are self-contradictory to varying degrees. In his classic work, *Steps to an Ecology of Mind*, Anthropologist Gregory Bateson used the term "double-bind[1]" to describe how we can drive each other crazy with conflicting messages we project about what we want.[2] Philosopher and psychologist William James concluded that craziness can be "the result of a belief system that is not working." Changing our concept of the world, he says, requires becoming "willing to change our belief system, let the past slip away, expand our sense of now, and dissolve the fear in our minds."[3]

What drives our confusion about the world? Often, the confusion is traceable to mixed messages received in early childhood, having to do with being able to feel safe. For example, a parent may make giving overt expressions of love contingent upon her child's conforming to exacting behavioral expectations. Being human, the child isn't likely to succeed at this 100 percent of the time. To train the child, the mother responds by withholding, despite the child's best efforts to please her mother. Mother and child come to view one another as disappointing, and even unloving and unlovable, ultimately resulting in a relationship in which needs remain unmet and closeness to another person is viewed as unreliable and dangerous.

Members of families that use this and other types of double-binds are likely to spend most of their resources on emotional survival. The patterns become absorbed into the individual's "operating system," and finally emerge in the personality configuration we call *self-irrelationship*—a double-bind *with oneself.* Over time, this state is consolidated by *brainlock*, the unconscious and neurobiological patterning behind the conviction that self-irrelationship is a true reflection of how the world is and how the individual needs to be in the world in order to survive. Having no insight into how this has come to be, the individual locks down her self-protective posture and throws away the key, making herself unable to recognize or even be curious about the world except through the filter of self-irrelationship.

Humans are able to identify needs and reflect on competing feelings and desires before deciding what actions to take, and, afterward, evaluate how well our choices worked. Neuropsychologist and psychoanalyst Mark Solms (2021, 117) states it point-blank: "We use emotions as a compass. It is feeling that guides all learning from experience." And so, if feelings and needs become dissociated as a result of anxiety, we're unable to use these inner "checks and balances" to make sense of experience either during or afterward. As a result, our memories are unreliable, our emotions poorly regulated, our sense of identity disrupted, and our relationships messy. We're not even able to be authentically "present" in any life situation. In short, dissociation is like a drug that buffers us from experiencing real life at the same time that it protects us from pain. What is dissociation? According to experts Elizabeth Howell and Sheldon Itzkowitz (2013, 125), dissociation is a last-ditch response to distress so intense it is impossible to make sense of what is happening, especially in childhood, when the brain is still developing and defense are immature. "[D]issociation occurs when the experience was so overwhelming that it could not be emotionally borne or consciously formulated. Dissociation refers to those gaps in memory, knowledge, and emotions that we don't know that we don't know—experience that was too overwhelming to be assimilated."The capacity to think reflectively, to create consistent meaning and sense of social reality, to generate a coherent autobiographical sense of self, loses out to simple survival, undermining the development of key life skills.

So—what's the answer? Can such problems be fixed by going into therapy to find a way to not be crazy? That's not how the authors see it. Instead, as with any other aspect of oneself, the sane approach is to accept and harness the reality of my crazy to make myself a more whole and effective person. This leads not only to better functioning, but to increased satisfaction with virtually everything about my life, including work and relationships. Perhaps most unexpectedly it leads to my finding myself living in a world that's more hospitable to who I *really* am and my unique kind of crazy.

Life's challenges teach us how to live. Turning to one another for love and support during difficult times makes for better, or at least more livable, outcomes. But without support, challenges can make us unmanageably crazy, leading to slow death. That isolated state is called *irrelationship*, and it fragments our relationship with others, with ourselves, and with our feelings and desires. *Self-irrelationship* leaves us unable to connect consciously with contradictory parts of ourselves and become able, thereby, to use them to improve our sense of well-being.

Self-irrelationship originates in our relationships with our first caregivers—usually mother and father. The attachment style we form with them shapes our relationships with ourselves. If this includes love, affection, gentleness, and firm but positive guidance, the result is likely to be a healthy relationship with oneself. However, a caregiver who is emotionally distant, or who targets the child with her or his own unmet needs and negative emotions, will leave the child prone to shame, insecurity, and self-neglect. Factors influencing this are both innate and learned, and can even result from epigenetic imprinting transmitted across generations.

We're born into a social ecology we don't control, but as we get older, we can learn to make discretionary decisions about how and with whom we live. This type of autonomy is what we, the authors, refer to as *making your crazy work for you*. If I don't learn the skill of making my crazy work for me, I'll probably remain trapped in irrelationship with myself and others.

Our earlier works—*Irrelationship* and *Relationship Sanity*—invite readers to figure out how irrelationship affects their interpersonal lives. A reader of one of our blog entries (https://www.psychologytoday.com/us/blog/irrelationship) raised questions about this that led to our writing this book, which represents our stepping back from the interpersonal into the intrapersonal:

> *How can I better understand irrelationship if I am single? Is there anything I can do as a single person to use the insight I've been attaining to prevent repeating irrelationship when I get back into a relationship? How does irrelationship play out when I'm single? What if I'm the only one in my relationship who thinks it is an irrelationship? Without being self-attacking, the question is, What's wrong with me that I keep ending up in these bad scenes, and what can I do to fix myself, before I get into more irrelationships with others?*

Unpacking Crazy

"What might this be?" is the classic question the analyst poses to the client taking the Rorschach inkblot test. The test is designed to elicit clues to defended secrets about ourselves that make us anxious and uncomfortable. Similarly, the term *crazy* in our title, *Making*

Your Crazy Work for You, is intended to prompt readers to reflect on questions such as

- What popped into your head when you saw the book's title?
- How do you define *crazy*?
- What's different about the crazy you feel in yourself and the crazy you see in others?
- What experiences with others have made you or them feel crazy?
- Do you feel down on yourself a lot of the time, and if so, why?
- What's the connection between your attitude toward yourself and your problems with others?

We've probably tipped our hand enough for readers to figure out that we view crazy as a tool for improving your approach to reality at the same time that you're feeling anxious or defensive. But learning to deliberately use this crazy can help you make better decisions in scary situations that will lead to healthier connections with others.

Crazy is sometimes a reaction to pain, fear, and anxiety. Couples' therapist Harville Hendrix (2008, 19–20) has said that

> If (a child's) caretakers can't figure out what is wrong, or if they withhold their attentions . . . the child experiences a primitive anxiety: the world is not a safe place. Since it has no way of taking care of itself and no sense of delayed gratification, it believes that getting the outside world to respond to its needs is truly a matter of life and death.

Going further, Masud Khan, a disciple of Donald Winnicott, describes this caretaking deficit as the failure of the "material protective shield."[4] When the caregiver doesn't protect the young child, her world will literally disintegrate, forcing her to work out her own survival scheme.

This book explores the outcome of this caretaking failure by showing how adoption of isolating protective mechanisms leads to insanity. However, relationship sanity can be built on unconditional self-acceptance. Without such embracing of self, "more flexible, complex, and integrated forms of relatedness may fail to emerge" (Boston Change Process Study Group 2019, 546).

"In life," the Boston Change Process Study Group continues, "there are special relationships with others that shape who we are and who we become" (540). Such relationships form the foundation of how we experience and know ourselves—specifically, how I know myself in all my parts. Since we are cultural and relational creatures, isolation is crazy and paradoxically makes me crazy by locking myself in with the rejection and abandonment I'm trying to avoid. At first glance, this state may look like a healthy independence and self-sufficiency but is actually the result of the delusion that separates us from our most indispensable resource: each other.[5] The first step toward others is to view my crazy as an opportunity for escaping the trap I've been living in.

As mentioned earlier, the quality of early caregiving is critical to preventing mental health problems (van Ijzendoorn et al. 1999; van der Kolk 2014). Being victimized by ineffective care resonates with psychiatrist Judith Herman's (1992, 92) perspective on early trauma: "When neither resistance nor escape is possible, the human system of self-defense becomes overwhelmed and disorganized. Each component of the ordinary response to danger, having lost its utility, tends to persist in an altered and exaggerated state long after the actual danger is over."

Irrelationship defends us from the anxiety caused by ineffective parental care. The child acts out this anxiety and seeks compensation by reversing roles with the caretaker.[6] When care isn't given out of love, the child learns to deal harshly with her or himself. This also creates divisions within the child that enable her to validate aspects of parental behavior such as providing food, shelter, and physical touch while ignoring (dissociating) behaviors such as criticism, abuse, or neglect. While this splitting may stabilize the child's world enough to allow her to focus on survival, she won't thrive or integrate any types of experience in a healthy way.

Reverse caretaking is both a compensation for and an enactment[7] of the dissociated[8] anxiety that masquerades as self-sufficiency, but which is actually the state of isolation and loneliness the authors equate with insanity, in which experiences of self are dissociated.[9] Thus the ineffective parental care we receive as a child is internalized, creating self-alienation[10] that shapes every decision, action, and outcome, while deadening one's experience of self.

According to traumatologist Bessel van der Kolk (2014, 3), "Trauma compromises the brain area that communicates the physical, embodied feeling of being alive." In the same volume, van der Kolk asserts that "(d)issociation prevents trauma from becoming integrated within the conglomerated, ever-shifting stores of autobiographical memory" (182). In other words, when overwhelmed by anxiety, experiences of self are so profoundly dissociated one from another that the individual is unable to recognize "me." Instead, cut off from self, other, and self–other, we vigilantly defend our dissociated self-states—states the interpersonal psychiatrist Harry Stack Sullivan (1953) describes as *not-me* states.[11]

Using this Book

The book is organized into three parts.

- **Part One: Identifying Your Crazy** looks at the basics of self-irrelationship and how it relates to early childhood experience and plays out in your everyday now.

- **Part Two: Treating Your Crazy** discusses intrapersonal approaches for undermining the deeply rooted blind spot that keeps you from seeing self-irrelationship for what it really is.

- **Part Three: Bending, Blending, and Mending** teaches techniques for engaging the "pushed aside" parts of who you really are as a means of building a whole, real life.

Our earlier books are designed primarily to be used by couples. This book, however, shows how irrelationship-based distancing affects my relationship with myself as well as with others. The *Staying on Target* exercises at the end of each chapter explore relationship history and what you think and experience *today* to assist in reconnecting with parts of yourself that you've put out of sight and out of mind. Reengaging with your crazy becomes the key to real connection with others.

PART I

IDENTIFYING YOUR CRAZY

CHAPTER ONE

How Self-Irrelationship Looks and Feels

Everybody brings different life-experience to their relationships, making all of us conceptualize and color our human interactions of every type differently. This is also true for the relationship with oneself. In the following section are examples of how self-irrelationship develops, looks, and binds us in real life as it shakes down along the lines of the following points, which are fleshed out in detail in our earlier books:

1. How self-irrelationship feels and how others respond to it.

2. How self-irrelationship affects all of our interactions with others.

3. How different parts of the individual interconnect, or don't, and how this shapes our perceptions of others and vice-versa.

4. The impact this has on our connection with the world.

Bind #1—The "Catch Me, F—k Me Over"

"I know it's kind of sick," Molly admitted. "But I kinda get off on how Jenny jerks us around to make us do what she wants."

Josh was taken aback. "You actually get off on that? She's so withholding—keeps things just out of our reach that we need to be able to even function around here. Then when we turn somersaults trying to meet her demands she acts like she's doing us a big fat favor by just showing up here and doing what she's supposed to be doing anyway. And no matter what we do, she always says something patronizing or even nasty about it while tripping on and on about what an expert she is in, well, every damn thing. It's ridiculous and infuriating, but, really, kinda sad at the same time."

"Yeah I know, Josh, but despite her bait-and-switch manipulation, I still love the project, so I'm willing to keep going with it, telling myself it's just a game, but with a great prize, if we can just get there. And anyway, if I don't talk that way to myself about it, I'll kill her."

"Well, I still don't get it."

"What? She's so emotionally destitute that it's easy to make her think that *we think* it's all about her, that without her, the whole thing would fall apart. So we'll do anything to keep her happy."

"But, Molly," said Josh, unconvinced, "isn't that exactly what we do?"

"Well, she obviously thinks so," said Molly, "And that's my game: that's what I've *wanted* her to think all along. So let her think she's got us where she wants us because I'm very sure that, when the time comes, we'll be able to turn the tables on her."

"I still don't get it."

This is an example of how irrelationship can look on the outside. But for the person in self-irrelationshp, the cat-and-mouse game is *with oneself*, and, along the way, with the world. It may *look* like a struggle to find the mate, job, or living situation that will make you "whole." But Molly is playing a game of manipulation in the context of professional work to cover up a more sinister game she's playing with herself to head off the risk of remembering the trauma she experienced as a child. And although it works, professionally, it also sidelines her conflicts about her identify and her value to others—conflicts so fundamental, that thinking about and "feeling" them is unacceptable. Meanwhile, this double bind has the added "benefit" of allowing her to ignore how she victimizes others.

As described earlier, self-irrelationship includes resistance to accepting anything others may offer us. In this sense, to be caught is to be "f—ked," i.e., cornered by the things self-irrelationship protects us from: 1) reliance on others, whom we fear will betray us as we were betrayed as small children; and 2) the feeling that we were hurt because we deserved it. For Molly, Jenny is a scapegoat onto whom she can project parts of herself that she rejects, which justifies her need for protection and for mistrusting Jenny. For people like Molly, life becomes a series of ultimately unsatisfactory (but addictive) relationships that keep blowing up, one way or another, but which also meet their need to avoid self-understanding by deflecting attention from themselves.

"Yeah, truth be told," continued Molly, "though I like the work we do and kind of enjoy the game, if I had the chance, I'd sink Jenny to the bottom."

Devaluing, and looking for ways to get rid of Jenny, is a ruse Molly uses as she keeps her eye on the exit, which is actually a way to sideline herself.

The flipside of self-irrelationship is the fear that accepting from others will require my reciprocation, and, down deep, I believe that I don't have anything of value to offer to others. The person who lives with this anxiety sees her life as a long line of unpaid debts, bad deals, and broken promises for which, sooner or later, she's going to be punished. The only sensible coping strategy, then, is isolation.

Bind #2—Trophy Kid

"I'm so proud of you."

Gary often said this to his twelve-year-old daughter Samantha, but it was the last thing she wanted to hear. Her whole sense of herself was built around her father reinforcing the importance of her always doing better and better at whatever she did. Maintaining her GPA and excelling at soccer left no room for stumbling, falling, or failing. As a result, Samantha usually felt the opposite of how she appeared—she was fragile and terrified of not being the best at everything she did.

Being made to walk that path can lead to catastrophic depression—what Freud (1914, 1958) describes in his paper on narcissism as "wrecked by success."[1] Mercilessly driven to excel, if Samantha encounters a situation in which she doesn't turn out to be "the best," her self-esteem and self-efficacy collapses. Children so driven are at risk for suicide if the image they project should ever be revealed to be a sham.

Close scrutiny of cases presented in our earlier published work reveals that in every case of irrelationship, self-irrelationship can be read between the lines. Two compulsive caregivers enacting their own anxiety together are actually living in the isolation of self-irrelationship. Drawn together unconsciously by histories of trauma, they live in conflict and flight from one another, never having developed skills for reflection or communication—skills necessary for working through conflict if they're ever going to be able to figure out whether they have anything in common besides the histories of trauma that drew them together in the first place.

Samantha doesn't find it easy to respond when her father tells her he's proud of her. She doesn't yet have enough self-understanding to see that her drive to achieve is a way of trying to make her father love her for *who she is*, rather than because of *what she does*. But she is beginning to realize that, in a way, her father's praise isn't about *her*. After a moment, she gave her customary response by rote: "Umm, thanks Daddy."

Samantha's parents met in college. When they graduated, her mother was pregnant, preempting their plans for grad school and comfortable professional lives. Her father took an entry-level job at an advertising firm, while her mother did freelance work and took online courses, which only partially made up for her resentment at being left alone to manage home and child care. Before long, they were actively blaming each other for their disappointment at how things had turned out. Heaping praise on Samantha became a way they could tell themselves and others that they harbored no bad feelings for their daughter interrupting their plans. They didn't knowingly set out to hijack Samantha's life, but that's what happened.

At first, Samantha interpreted being called "special" as praise. But as she worked harder and harder to keep up with her parent's expectations, she became increasingly unforgiving of herself if she felt she fell short. Her "specialness" took on a dark meaning as she increasingly took responsibility for her parents' feelings about her or anything else. In short, Samantha enacted a compulsive caretaking routine with her parents, increasingly trapping herself in a state of self-irrelationship, driven to prove her specialness to everyone she met.

One day when her father facetiously asked her (as he often did) how it felt to be a "trophy kid," Samantha fleetingly saw herself as a performing animal who was supposed to distract her mother and father from their hatred of each other and their life together. Samantha didn't herself feel hated, but she somehow knew she wasn't loved for herself, regardless of the tricks she performed. Invested as she was in her caretaking, it didn't even give her pause—it was almost all she knew.

"It sucks," she replied.

Her father silently congratulated himself for his daughter's clever sense of humor: "Just like her old man."

Bind #3—Betrayal

Betrayal adds a powerful element to trauma, rending it more destructive than trauma without betrayal. Psychologist Jennifer Freyd defines "betrayal trauma" as follows:

> Betrayal trauma occurs when the people or institutions on which a person depends for survival significantly violate that person's trust or well-being: Childhood physical, emotional, or sexual abuse perpetrated by a caregiver are examples of betrayal trauma. When psychological trauma involves betrayal, the victim may be less aware or less able to recall the traumatic experience because to do so will likely lead to confrontation or withdrawal by the betraying caregiver, threatening a necessary attachment relationship and thus the victim's survival.

Thus, betrayal trauma is the ultimate double-bind in the sense that survival and intimate abuse come face-to-face. Becoming blind is the last resort, one with consequences. Betrayal trauma is associated with higher rates of PTSD, depression, impaired emotional awareness, and poorer physical well-being. In addition, adults with betrayal trauma have difficulty recalling childhood maltreatment, a dissociative response called "betrayal blindness."

Furthermore, early betrayal trauma—compared with abuse and neglect without betrayal—is associated with significantly higher chances of future traumatization (Gobin & Freyd 2009, 243). Those with childhood betrayal trauma are four to five times more likely to be revictimized in adolescence and adulthood, believed to be related to the impact of both dissociative responses like betrayal blindness, which make it hard to sense and respond to dangerous individuals, as well as due to the tendency to misread others' motives and interpersonal interactions. Being too tolerant of betrayal, even when we do see it, relates to the emotional numbing that typically goes along with unresolved trauma, leaving us vulnerable to ill-intentioned others. Learning to see betrayal when it is present and yet not perceive it to be there, by contrast, is liberating—empowering, creating more choices as our trust radar becomes more robust and refined.

More on Origins of Self-Irrelationship: With or To?

Irrelationship is an adaptation constructed *with* another person, though at first it may look like it's done *to* them. It's a response to the anxiety-provoking environment of early childhood, which created a split in the individual between child and earliest caregiver that prevents development of self-knowledge and the ability to know others. In the case of self-irrelationship, a similar split prevents an individual from encountering various aspects of herself. If this rift isn't addressed and healed, the experience of her own humanity and feelings is out of reach. Encounters with others are, therefore, tolerable only through irrelationship.

Our earlier work (Borg, Brenner, and Berry 2015, 2017, 2018) describes development of reverse-caretaking in one of two ways:

1. The *Performer* role, in which the individual fixes, rescues, or cures the distressed caregiver, or

2. The *Audience* role, in which we contrive behavioral or relational patterns that allow the caregiver to believe that her or his poor caregiving is effective.

The pattern developed between child and caregiver in irrelationship is called their *song-and-dance routine*. These routines usually start out as a rudimentary form of the *human antidepressant*[2]—an adaptation in which the child relieves his own anxiety by taking on behaviors intended to make the parent or other caregiver feel less unhappy. We go into a great deal of detail in Chapters Three and Four to describe some of what we see as the most typical ways that song-and-dance routines manifest as caretaking behaviors, we call these GRAFTS. In a nutshell, GRAFTS are a set of very common song-and-dance routines in children that are expressed when the child becomes identified with and entrenched in behaviors—that become personality characteristics—that come to define (and confine) the child as one of the following:

- Good
- Right
- Absent
- Funny
- Tense
- Smart

Self-irrelationship acts out anxiety by either dominance or dependence. It plays out through the individual's seeking control over himself; however, unlike a scenario involving others, the power struggle within the individual has no target for his caregiving behaviors other than himself. He therefore has no means of escaping himself except through self-obliterating behaviors such as fabricating a false life, retreating into addiction, or even committing suicide. This individual's overwhelming need is to control the environment, emotional or actual, by *mood-tuning*, which is a fancy clinical term for recruiting others to help him manage the world by participating in the song-and-dance routine he uses to blot out his awareness of how vulnerable and anxious he is.

Our clinical practice and research have led us to conclude that, for individuals who suffered childhood trauma, a whole experience of self-and-other is created through a process of rupture and repair rather than by inducing perfect attunement in others. This is supported by the findings of infant researchers Edward Tronick (1989, 2007) and Janine Sternberg (2018).[3] "Good enough" is far more useful to our psychological health than an impossible search for perfection. Every misstep can thus be viewed as an opportunity for choosing growth and building relationship sanity, that healthy balance of giving and receiving in a relationship. Opting for relationship sanity may look insane, because it asks the individual to suspend disbelief, step back from knee-jerk reactions, and deliberately enlist distressing feelings (i.e., craziness) as a tool for self-connection and self-learning.

The rupture-and-repair process is key to becoming open to oneself and allowing the other *in*.[4] Feeling safe in any relationship requires compassion for oneself and others. *Compassionate empathy* is the gateway to overcoming entrenched routines that reinforce a negative conception of myself. Compassion does not know "self" or "other." Instead, it reveals the anxiety-producing "other" *within* ourselves. Such self-care is initiated simply by allowing myself to believe that I'm as entitled to care as anyone. This shift can undermine compulsive caregiving, masochistic self-sacrifice, and isolating self-sufficiency.

In *The Body Keeps the Score,* traumatologist Bessel van der Kolk (2014, 81) says, "Being able to feel safe with other people is probably the single most important aspect of mental health: safe connections are fundamental to meaningful and satisfying lives." Living in an unsafe world as a child is traumatic and a chronic crisis (Borg 2003). As the child matures, his response to this state may include an almost addictive dependence on serial crises and on destructive relationships that result from inability to exercise good judgment even when making major life decisions.

Song-and-dance routines are imperfect copies of childhood dysfunction. Our earlier work explores what this looks like in our relations with others, but a similar pattern plays out within the individual's own mind, with the analogous purpose of protecting her from anxiety created by her own feelings and actions. This splitting within oneself[5] leaves gaps that are full of potential for change but which, if left unattended, make us "crazy." In more profound cases, we are split into part-selves that "live in the same house," occasionally passing near each other from time to time but refusing acknowledgment of one another.

Psychoanalyst Harold Searles (1979) believed that a child's first job in life is to provide therapy to his primary caregiver—usually the mother. He feels that his survival depends on how well his mother takes care of him.[6] So any distress on his mother's part may be so intolerable that he'll do anything to make her feel better, i.e., to relieve her craziness. Bion (1962) says one of the mother's major functions is to enable the child to manage the chaotic disagreeable sensations such as hunger, physical discomfort, and confusion about his own body and mind by creating a container the young mind can use to organize such experiences without falling to pieces. This "apparatus for thinking" enables coping with any challenges to body or mind. The child who doesn't develop this skill is at risk for becoming overly self-sufficient, a principal marker of irrelationship.

In self-irrelationship, a similar dynamic is acted out internally; only we enact our own "helpful behavior" to escape anxiety and preserve sanity by contriving a plausible sense of self and the world. Unfortunately, this maladaptive response also numbs creative parts of oneself, which, as mentioned above, is a barrier to a full experience of oneself and of life generally. It also blocks our ability to work through the trauma that created the anxiety to begin with, leading to developmental delays including persistence into adulthood of negative childhood patterns.

The behaviors resulting from this pattern are some of the most familiar buzzwords of pop-psychology:

- Self-sabotage
- Codependency
- Moral masochism
- Compulsive caregiving

The following is a simple way of framing what self-irrelationship looks like.

In self-irrelationship:

- I avoid taking care of myself, or I do so only under duress and in a way that feels as if I'm only going through the motions.

- I don't feel that I'm good enough. Either I have a piece missing, I'm not connected with something important about myself, or I feel a deep dissatisfaction with myself that I can't put into words.

From this perspective, irrelationship is created by two people in self-irrelationship. Until each individual addresses the underlying trauma, their craziness works against them. As an example of how that works, we'll take a look at Glen, who was one half of the "Patient Zero Couple" spotlighted in our first book, *Irrelationship*.

Self-Irrelationship: Performer to Yourself as Audience: A Shrink's Song-and-Dance Routine[7]

Glen, a forty-two-year-old psychologist, went into therapy because of feelings that his practice had bogged down. However, in therapy, he came to realize that his feelings of failure arose from failing to satisfy his most critical Audience: himself.

When Glen's parents' marriage failed, he almost immediately took responsibility for how well or how poorly his mother coped with the disappointment and depression that followed the divorce. Through various song-and-dance routines, when he repeatedly failed to relieve her distress, he continually ramped up his efforts to make her feel better, but always with the same outcome. A residual effect of this "failure" was that it left him feeling chronically inadequate and desperate to prove to himself and others what a good guy he was. Therapy helped him to understand how he had acted out his feelings of failure with his mother. But the more complicated task was coming to understand how his taking on the burden of fixing others had blinded him to his own dissociated emotions and memories from childhood. In other words, he *got it*, interpersonally, but not as it applied to his relationship with himself. In fact, Glen's laser-sharp focus on others' relationships was his most powerful tool for blocking self-reflection and recovering the disowned parts of himself, a.k.a. *self-irrelationship.*

Borg (2003) writes:

> In pure war cultures—that is, in cultures that enact a perpetual preparation for war—the notion of peace is itself a defensive fantasy, although to survive psychically we distract ourselves from such frightening stimuli as widespread terrorist activities and other events that demonstrate our pure war status. Pure war obliterates the distinction between soldier and citizen. We have all been drafted (58).

Similarly, when the individual recognizes his capacity for total annihilation, the distinction between "soldier and citizen" disappears. Internal dialogue is squelched and a state of pure war snatches up all available resources to maintain the fantasy of peace.

For Glen, discovering self-irrelationship meant traversing a boundary that was guarded by his perplexity. To transition from isolation to acceptance and self-love first required grasping a seemingly self-absorbed perspective that, for Glen, was associated with selfishness and incompetent parenting. As he became comfortable with the idea of lovingly viewing himself as an "other" who was entitled to be protected and nurtured—an idea foreign to his upbringing—he became able to unpack and embrace an authentic relationship with himself *and* with the crazy of his denying his own feelings and needs.

Helping Hands: Glen and Maurice

During his therapy sessions, Glen frequently brought up his own clients who were in analysis. This was a set up for "transference-countertransference enactments," a process wherein dynamics of early caretaking relationships are played out in current relationships. In analysis, this process, wherein one's history *is* transferred into a current relationship, is often so highly charged that it blurs or crosses professional boundaries. Glen used it as an irrelationship song-and-dance routine by making patients into peers as a way of being "helpful." The reality, however, was that, by doing this, he deprived them of the opportunity to use him appropriately in his therapeutic role—including, especially, allowing them to contribute to him in any significant or meaningful way. In one such case, Glen borrowed his patient Maurice's dreams as his own and presented it to his therapist:

> We were at some gala garden party. I think it was in your backyard at that summer place you own in the Hamptons. We were just sort of mingling together, you and I, in the grass when this large man approached. I thought maybe he was your father—maybe Wotan from the Ring Cycle, you know, Wagner. Suddenly, there appeared in the garden this grand stage, and the final immolation scene from Götterdämmerung is being performed onstage. Grand scale, and then suddenly you, the man, maybe your . . . father, no, too young . . . are on stage . . . No, we are beyond onstage, we are traveling through the whole of the Ring Cycle . . . We are traveling to Valhalla. The journey is treacherous; we have to hold hands . . . The man leads the way, he grasps your hand and you grasp mine, this is the only way we can make it. We finally do make it to Valhalla, enter the throne room to feast with all the fallen heroes. We sit down, the three of us, and for some reason the man and I begin to attempt to feed you, (Dr. Glen). However, each time that one of us puts food on our utensils, you pull out this very sharp blade and slice off our fingers over and over again. Each time you sever my fingers, or that guy's, they grow back, there's more food on the fork, and whop—you slice our fingers right off our hands.

Glen couldn't get Maurice's dream out of his head. He didn't have a house in the Hamptons, but he did feel a deep emotional resonance with Brunnhilde's famous "Immolation Scene" at the end of Götterdämmerung.

Maurice was Glen's first patient at a mental health clinic in New York City, to which he had been referred following a psychiatric hospitalization. Maurice also loved Wagnerian opera, including *Götterdämmerung*. As Glen became increasingly interested in psychoanalytic training, Maurice became increasingly willing to "help" him. Predictably, this devolved into a role-reversal in which Maurice became Glen's compulsive caretaker, with the twist that, each time Maurice explicitly offered caregiving, Glen resisted (cut off his fingers). Maurice's dream mirrored this dynamic of each rebuffing what the other offered. Before long, Maurice's treatment stagnated because neither allowed himself to see and own up to what was happening between them. In loose reference to a once-popular song Maurice loved, they could stab at it forever, but they *could not kill the beast* (i.e., treat Maurice's clinical issues). In classic irrelationship terms, failure to address the beast led to dissociated anxiety and weaponized caretaking.

Working Through

Similar dynamics surfaced near the end of Glen's marriage to his first wife, Vicky, when he turned to her for support during this traumatic period. For her, Glen's admission of vulnerability was the deal-breaker for their collaborative caretaking marriage, and she fled. His experience with Maurice was something of a tip-off for Glen, but Vicky's leaving their marriage forced him to examine his compulsive caretaking role and how it distanced him from his own needs and desires.

Glen's irrelationship routine came with a high back-loaded cost, beginning with Maurice, who brought home to him that the two of them were entrenched in transferential reactions—repeating dynamics that brought each person's traumatic history into their current interaction—to Glen's self-irrelationship-based therapist role and the expectations that came with it.

Glen's countertransference reaction was to feel injured, and resentful, as well as ineffective and lonely (his crazy). Analysis, however, excavated the primary expectation underlying his compulsive caretaking—the same that he had placed on his mother, his wife, and his other patients: "Get well, get out, and take your craziness with you!" Fortunately, this backfired against Glen, pushing him to confront the irrelationship basis of his personal and professional relationships and find his way to realistic expectations in both arenas.

In therapy, Glen gradually came to understand his caretaking of his mother and his anger at her for not getting better. Over time this became a dark rage whose existence he denied for decades. Others, however, saw it demonstrated dramatically in fistfights with his brother, abruptly dropped romantic attachments, and ruined family celebrations such as his mother's second wedding. When a professional crisis finally drove him into therapy, he had become willing to explore how he had adapted to childhood trauma by creating splits within himself. That's the point at which his crazy began work for him.

The Bait and Switch: Self-Irrelationship as Anti-Anxiety Technique

When I blind myself to my emotional life as Glen did, I dissociate from crucial self-experience, complicating my ability to respond to my feelings in a constructive way. I may spend years trying to convince myself that I'm smart or clever enough to find my way through emotionally complicated situations, but a fundamental fact of our humanity is that you can't outthink your feelings.[8]

It's tempting to try to look strong when wanting to impress someone. But if I always make a point of looking totally in control even when I'm terrified, I put a barrier between my own and others' actual experience of me. This will interfere increasingly with my ability to create balanced relationships of any kind—personal, professional, or romantic. I'll end up in an emotional straitjacket I'm afraid to remove. To make matters worse, I probably won't realize what a bad idea this is until it begins to crack, and feelings I've been trying to keep under wraps start seeping out in unexpected ways.

Self–Other Help

Self–Other Help is an innovative paradigm for life change, distinct from the well-known self-help paradigm. Applied to self-irrelationship, Self–Other Help creates a safe space for vulnerability, truth-telling, and interactive repair that allows me to be who I really am, opening the way for an accepting, loving relationship with myself.

Re-owning split-off parts of myself (my crazy) also reduces my self-sufficiency delusion so that I can embrace:

- Who I really am.

- What I have to give.

- What others can offer me.

- My need both to give and receive.

In other words, this process cracks my isolation and moves me toward relationship sanity *with myself.*

The Key Ingredient of Self–Other Help

Empathy is like a powerful electrical source, while *compassion* is the regulator that protects me from electrocution. Glen was afraid that accepting help from others would make him unsafe. Deciding to allow himself to be helped by his therapist initiated the momentous cracking open of his brainlock and giving up of his caretaking routine. Without this shift, instead of taking in his therapist's caregiving, he would have terminated therapy as their approach to his reservoir of rage drove up his anxiety level. Instead, however, the way of compassionate empathy gradually cleared a space in which he could feel safe calling the denied parts of himself and his past by their proper names.

Song-and-Dance Routines

Irrelationship theory is grounded in Harold Searles's hypothesis that human beings are natural-born caregivers.[9] John Bowlby (1958), the progenitor of attachment theory, found that human beings have an inborn motivation to be *care-seekers*.[10] We have an innate desire to heal the wounds of those around us—especially those of the primary caregivers on whom we depend for security and comfort.[11]

In self-irrelationship, the irrelationship dynamic is played out *within oneself*: the "Performer" element of self acts out routines designed to convince the internal "Audience" that he doesn't need other people—a delusion sprung from the conviction that the most dependable truth about one's primary caregivers is that they can't be trusted.

Psychoanalyst Erich Fromm (1956) wrote, "Giving is the highest expression of potency. In the very act of giving, I experience my strength, my wealth, and my power . . . Giving is more joyous than receiving, not because it is a deprivation, but because in the act of giving lies the expression of my aliveness."[12] The contrivance of self-sufficiency deprives me of the self-fulfilling pleasure of giving and taking essential to whole human experience.

According to van der Kolk (2014, 112), "(M)astering the skill of self-regulation depends to a large degree on how harmonious our early interactions with our caregivers are." The basic explanation is that when a child's caregiver is emotionally unavailable (and we pick up on this from a very early age), the child feels unsafe and will do anything to feel safe again. This is because the caregiver is the child's entire reality. So he develops actions and behaviors (a song-and-dance routine) intended to elicit reassurance from the caregiver. These routines may include being "good," "smart," "tough," "funny," "silly," "strong"—whatever it takes to make Mom pay attention to him. Once the kid figures out an effective routine, he uses it whenever necessary. As he gets older he'll continue to use the same routine on pretty much everybody he encounters, to keep his world comfortable and safe—that is, until something happens to make him realize that for some reason it's not working the way it used to. The type of caretaking behavior the individual adopts is influenced by his temperament and the techniques available.

Here are some examples of what these anxiety-relieving routines might look like as the child matures:

- If being "good" worked with my mom, I made a point of being "good" with everyone, even when the "good" behavior worked against my own best interests.

- If my mom seemed amused when I made a point of being "funny," I became the class clown, and later the comedian who was always "on" in social situations—especially in times of heightened stress. This also distracted me from any distress I might be feeling.

- If my caregiver liked it when I kept quiet, out of the way, and never made demands, I went through life keeping a low profile and neglecting my own needs.

- If my mom seemed to like that I "stayed strong" in difficult situations, I made a point of appearing strong and "together" in all kinds of situations, never asking for help, and never letting myself depend on others for anything.

- If acting "smart" pleased my mom, I made sure I looked and sounded "smart" about everything—especially in front of others. Only, by doing this, I cut myself off from benefiting from others' experience and expertise. This also had the effect of preempting the exploration of interests of my own.

Taking on one or another of these routines ultimately deprives me of life choices, while paradoxically allowing me to believe I'm in control of my life and can manage just fine without others.

Shunting aside genuine connection with others and with my own experience in these ways is likely to confuse my relationship with my own character and personality. What does this look like in a person's life?

Simon's parents fought constantly, and his siblings were brutally competitive with one another. He described his father as a workaholic, while his mother constantly suffered from apparently psychosomatic illnesses (she actually died from one of her illnesses when Simon was fourteen). Though materially comfortable, their family life was fragmented by emotional distance, illness, and disability. Nevertheless, they colluded to project an image of harmony and stability that conveyed to the outside world that everything was "okay" in their household.

This joint but unconscious facade provided space for every family member to develop a means of "self-caretaking." While this may seem a reasonable adaptation under the circumstances, it separated them even further from one another, leaving them less able to name and deal with the pain they shared. The result was that each retreated into a delusion of self-sufficiency. They continued to act as if they contributed to family life, but each was, in fact, carefully screened from having to risk giving or receiving from one another.

The self-care that Simon practiced was so effective that, despite his history of trauma, he became a highly successful professional. In his public persona, Simon was regarded as an affable and focused high-achiever. The private Simon, who was known to few, could be humorous and creative. Known to even fewer was a Simon who, when threatened, became protective and aggressive.

As he moved into middle age, Simon became increasingly aware of these discrete parts of himself, and also came to realize that the image of competence he projected was a relic of the "everything's okay" performance his family took up when he was a kid. The self-care he'd used to keep himself "safe" within his family was actually his part in the facade of "okay" his family projected. Harder to grasp was that this artificiality cut him off from meaningful connection with anyone—family, friends, business associates. In short, the result of his family's adaptation was that it isolated him from experiences that could—or threatened to—reveal his own humanity to himself.

I Ain't Got It

"Whenever somebody tries to help me with something—with anything at all, actually—the first thing out of my mouth, no matter what's going on, is, 'It's okay, I've got it.'"

Kristy was discussing her typical knee-jerk reaction to others' offers of help with her therapist. It's reminiscent of a scene from Mel Brooks's 1997 movie *High Anxiety,* in which Dr. Thorndyke (Brooks) is met at the airport by his assistant. The assistant repeatedly tries to lift Dr. Thorndyke's trunk, insisting, "I got it! I got it! I got it!" before dropping it to the ground, panting, "I ain't got it."

Affectation of self-sufficiency, even to the point of superheroism or martyrdom, is a telltale symptom of irrelationship with oneself.

"But," Kristy protested, "I always thought self-sufficiency was a good thing. I've always wanted to be admired for being an independent woman who doesn't need to lean on anyone. But now that we're talking about it, I'm starting to wonder if that's why I've always felt not quite connected with my boyfriends—or anybody else, if I'm gonna be honest about it."

Few things make us feel valued like being asked for help—being given the opportunity to be useful and feel needed. The most powerful weapon against my delusion of self-sufficiency is to ask someone else to give me a hand.

Kristy continued, "Whenever anybody offers to help me with something, anything, I can feel myself starting to panic."

When mired in irrelationship, offers of assistance from others tap into my old fears that if I say yes, I'll be exposing vulnerability, which is perilously close to allowing intimacy. This kind of self-shielding expands upon Wilhelm Reich's (1933, 1980) notion of *character armor,* which refers to the use of the full range of psychological defense (Borg 2003). It defends me by blocking my consciousness of my anxiety. However, even if I'm unaware of it, I'll enact that anxiety behaviorally with whoever is making me anxious, even if that person is only trying to get a little closer to me.

"I had no clue I was protecting myself from what I wanted, or thought I wanted, from others. I thought I was just 'being nice' by not being any trouble to others. And, well, it does seem to have backfired, because after a while everybody just started leaving me alone."

That insight—realizing the I *don't* got it—can be the beginning of the end of isolation, simply by not keeping everybody away from my "crazy."

Self-Irrelationship and Depression

Depression is an important part of the self-irrelationship picture. As the name suggests, depression is a lowering of mood that, to be treated properly, calls for careful evaluation. In our culture, this is complicated by the widespread perception that any unhappy feeling may legitimately be labeled "depression."

Clinicians sometimes mistake grief for depression if they don't take a proper history, often failing to identify significant loss. Ongoing neglect of this part of a person's history can result in ongoing, cumulative continuation of trauma that began with the early child-caregiver relationship. Another possible complication is that the individual may be enlisting depression to defend against such anxiety. For these reasons, clinicians view depression as a "state" rather than a "feeling." A not-so-obvious implication is that someone entangled in self-irrelationship may "feel depressed" because her routine of helping, fixing, and saving others is no longer keeping the lid on her anxiety. Breakthrough of anxiety may be the needed indicator to make her willing to use her crazy as a tool for relieving her long-standing discomfort.

How Does Self-Irrelationship Affect My Life and Relationships?

Like irrelationship, self-irrelationship manages anxiety with scripted routines that are used to prevent my having to reconcile contradictory parts of myself. The contradictions can be dramatic: I may project puffed-up ideas of myself, but I'm so emotionally fragile that minor slights from others send me into a paroxysm of rage or pain. I'm likely to be perfectionistic in my self-expectations, even though I know I can't live up to them. I may have the same kinds of emotional needs that others do. All in all, no matter what I do or don't do, I feel a deep emotional pain I'm afraid to label and unable to relieve.

The Slovenian cultural theorist Slavoj Žižek (2009, 40) provides insight into why we buy into self-irrelationship: "The experience we have of our lives from within, the story we tell ourselves about ourselves in order to account for what we are doing, is a lie—the truth lies rather outside, in what we do." For William James, "(t)he greatest revolution of our generation is the discovery that human beings, by changing the inner attitudes of their minds, can change the outer aspects of their lives."[13]

In self-irrelationship, our truth requires decoding and translation, much as a child tries to figure out how to get her mother to take care of her properly. The resulting unconscious reverse-caregiving pact between child and parent turns into a trap that may never be discovered.

Žižek (2008, 22) encapsulates their relationship: "I want you not only to do what I want, but to do it as if you really want to do it—I want to regulate not only what you do, but also your desires. The worst thing that you can do, even worse than not doing what I want you to do, is to do what I want you to do without wanting to do it."

This feeling of power over a parent can at first be exhilarating. But as the child becomes increasingly gratified by the delusion that he has the power to make others happy, he will gradually disappear from his proper role in life. Oddly, in so doing he loses the ability even to make himself happy.

STAYING ON TARGET

Self-Compassion Scale

Understanding where you are with self-compassion, and keeping track of developing self-compassion, is key for healing and personal growth. There are many evidence-based benefits associated with increased compassion, including improvements in mood, anxiety, and post-traumatic symptoms, as well as forming the basis for proper self-care and self-parenting as part of overall wellness. Please take a few minutes now to consider your own self-compassion using validated approaches.

There are many ways to measure self-compassion. We encourage you to visit https://self-compassion.org/test-how-self-compassionate-you-are/. There you can access psychologist Kristin Neff's research-based test, "How Self-Compassionate Are You?" as well as other self-compassion scales and practices to try.

Exercise
Dysfunctional Behaviors Used to Quiet Anxiety

The table below lists anxiety-blocking behaviors, who performs them and why, who they target, and what their effect is.

Dysfunctional Behavior	Who Used the Behavior and Why	Target/ Recipient of Behavior and Impact	Song-and-Dance Routine I Devised to Fix
Speaking disparagingly about neighbors, comparing them to our family.	Mother. To distract from family issues by creating negative feelings toward others.	All family members. Isolates us from neighbors.	I become "negotiator" between my family and neighbors to excuse parents' behavior while promoting tolerance for neighbors.

Dysfunctional Behavior	Who Used the Behavior and Why	Target/ Recipient of Behavior and Impact	Song-and-Dance Routine I Devised to Fix
Ignoring parents' drug use.	Daughters. To maintain image of stable family/ household. Allows parents to avoid awareness of impact of drug use on our family.	All family members, neighbors, friends and teachers. Allows personal care and other needs to remain unmet. Interferes with school work. Social isolation.	Covering for parents by lying to teachers and others about their erratic behavior.

Using the table as a guide, analyze your significant relationships:

- What dysfunctional behaviors in yourself, past and present, can you identify that affect how you relate to others today?

- What relationship do you see between these behaviors and the way you were or weren't cared for as a child?

- What behaviors do you see in others that you think they may be using to keep from getting too close to others?

- What connection do you see between your family history and the way you interact or avoid interacting with others?

- What connection do you see between how you protect yourself and things in your environment that make you uneasy?

CHAPTER TWO

Brainlock 101:
Why We Become Stuck

Irrelationship song-and-dance routines develop in brain, body, and mind at the interpersonal, intrapersonal, and intrapsychic levels. This is because the dynamics of interpersonal relations become our operating system, leading to repetition of irrelationship patterns both within oneself and with others. Its purpose is to control connections with others to so that they don't include emotional investment and vulnerability. The song-and-dance routine is also a place we hide from our own feelings so that connection with others is impossible.

Brainlock is the term for psychological and even physiological changes that enforce this disconnect. But the term also denotes how the individual protects himself from anxiety he initially felt as a child as a result of an unpredictable environment, but later in life it sidelines spontaneity, denies vulnerability, and disallows transparency and openness.

"Same Brain Every Day"

"Every day I wake up in the same brain, and every day turns out to be just as disappointing as the day before."

Genie was describing disappointments at romance to her therapist, who is one of this book's authors.

"I don't think it's what I'm looking for, but everybody I go out with turns out to be pretty much the same guy. It's always exciting at first because they *seem* like boyfriend material—kinda like the excitement of eating at the new restaurant everybody's talking about but never getting past the cocktails. And then, when I get home, I feel as if I wasted another evening eating white bread."

Like all living creatures, human beings tend toward homeostasis, which is just a fancy way of saying that all our systems are programmed to keep things on an even keel, or if something disturbs the equilibrium, begins immediately to restabilize it. Something like this is also true of our connections with others— family, friends, coworkers, and even large social and political systems. According to social scientists, maintaining stability is a natural part of being human.

"Of course, I'm always excited about dating somebody new. And if the guy is busy or seems hesitant, that just makes me go for it even harder. But the weird part is that the minute a guy lets me know he's interested in me, I start having second thoughts—I suddenly see things about him that I don't like or I think don't measure up. So even before we've gone on our first date, I've already started looking for an excuse to cancel or just call it all off."

What happens with Genie is what brainlock looks like. My commitment to getting close to somebody is almost—but not quite— as ingrained as my commitment to avoiding it. In this case, Genie maintains homeostasis—stability—by controlling how close she allows others to get. Her complaining to her therapist that she always finds herself going out with the same guy, with the same outcome, shows that it's not working so well anymore, and that she might just be ready to look more closely at what's happening and change it.

"Am I deliberately doing this to *myself* without even realizing it?" she asked her therapist.

"Well," he answered, "It seems like you've gotten good at sniffing out guys who *might* fit with your idea of husband material, but before you dare let yourself find out, you've started talking yourself into showing them the door." Her therapist paused, then asked, "Can you think of anyone whose marriage might have given you reason to think marriage may not be such a good idea?"

"Are you kidding? You know what a lousy marriage my mom and dad had. They were constantly threatening to either leave or lock the other one out. Whenever they'd fight, I'd get so scared I'd hide, and then I was afraid they'd get so mad that they'd forget all about me and just leave me." Genie's eyes began to fill with tears. "I didn't know *what* to do. I remember wondering if it would help if I was *extra* good so they wouldn't *want* to leave. I remember I'd stay in my room as much as I could so that I didn't do anything to make them blow up. But nothing I did made any difference. They just kept fighting."

Genie had never quite stopped wondering if something she had done was responsible for how bad things were in her home. This created an apprehensiveness in her about being close to others that she had never been able to work through. So she never allowed herself to get really close to anyone—romantic interests or anyone else. In other words, she never allowed the "unknown quantity" of another person to get close enough to challenge her fragile homeostasis.

The therapeutic approach to Genie's self-irrelationship, for that is what this was, was for her to learn to feel safe being truthful—first with herself, then with others—about her fear of getting close, and then to use exactly that part of herself as the basis for a new homeostasis, a *genuine* stability built on unconditional acceptance of *who she really is*. Without such self-acceptance, intimacy will remain out of reach.

A Closer Look at Brainlock

According to van der Kolk (2014, 34), "The social environment interacts with brain chemistry." He goes on to say that the "most important job of the brain is to ensure our survival, even under miserable conditions . . . and since we human beings are mammals, creatures that can only survive and thrive in groups, all of [the brain's functions] require coordination and collaboration" (55).

As we have now seen, the mind protects itself from trauma both by splitting of self-and-other and by splitting of self. Brainlock develops as a *preemptive* response to the threat of possible future interactions, much as it develops in response to actual personal interactions that may call for self-disclosure.

Neurobiological, Interpersonal, and Social-Contextual Components of Brainlock

A little neuroscience goes a long way, and this emerging field, as much as we know, leaves much more undiscovered. So we want to be careful not to overuse biological explanations while at the same time recognizing their growing importance, along with genetic and epigenetic factors. We focus mostly on developmental influence, largely socially learned factors that shape who we are through interactions with the environment, including other people. However, as the saying goes, "Genetics loads the gun; environment pulls the trigger."

With that in mind, a brief look at some of the influences may be useful—influences that are a combination of nature and nurture. What might this look like in real life? Well, a person may be born with low oxytocin activity, making them less responsive to a caregiver, and perhaps contributing to a tendency to maintain distance in relationships, as seems to be evident in autistic children. This genetic predisposition may be amplified in persons with a detached caregiver. On the other hand, someone with a responsive, warm caregiver is more likely to develop deeper and more connected relationships with others.

While development continues throughout adulthood, early intervention has the greatest impact on developmental trajectory. The approaches we discuss can stimulate changes ongoing in the biological and social areas.

Neurobiological Factors: Putting the "Brain" in "Brainlock"

Brain science is still pretty new, but promising. When working on personal development and relationships satisfaction, a little bit of understanding goes a long way. While we don't want to oversimplify, consideration of basic neurobiological influences shaping and shaped by our experience provides a place to begin self-reflection and change. To help with that, the following list is a brief overview of common neurotransmitters involved in bonding, motivation, and mood; how neural networks shape experience and perception; and the emerging role of hereditary influences that our response to life experiences, including stress.

- Oxytocin: A neuropeptide ("short protein") brain hormone involved in: 1) mother-infant bonding and breastfeeding; 2) romantic pair bonding; and 3) "prosocial" functions such as empathy, compassion, and altruism. Elevated oxytocin levels are associated with close bonding and increased drive to care for another at one's own expense (Acevedo et al. 2011; Carter 2014).

- Dopamine: The "reward" neurotransmitter. Dopamine is involved in reinforcing repetitive behaviors, even to the point of addiction and compulsion. It also mediates "internal reward" circuit activity for regular and adaptive routines and repetitive behaviors. High dopamine levels are seen in both partners of relationships that include a compulsive quality. The high levels of reward activity mediated by dopamine are putatively required to balance the high levels of pain associated with unmet needs (deprivation) and with repetitive negative experiences related to unsuccessful attempts to "fix" things (punishment) (Love 2014).

- Other neuro-factors. Vasopressin: the "male" version of oxytocin, associated with courtship and mating. Glutamate: the key "excitatory" neurotransmitter, which increases brain activity (balanced by GABA, the key "inhibitory" neurotransmitter in the brain). Endogenous opioids, i.e., "pleasure" hormones (Insel 2010). Other factors could be discussed, but the primary message is that irrelationship experience is mediated by an array of biological and biologically related factors.

- Neural networks: The brain, like the internet, functions as a set of interconnected networks, ideally working together to form a coherent sense of self and world. Trauma disrupts network activity so that the "executive control network" becomes disconnected from emotional brain systems, leading to dysregulation and dissociation, while simultaneously hyperconnected with the "salience network," which tunes the mind to scan for threats similar to past traumas, interfering with ordinary working memory. Attention in the moment is disrupted by memories from the past and by strong emotional experience that's disconnected from context. The brain's resting state, or "default mode network," gets disrupted by intrusions of "absent memory" affecting decision-making and conflict resolution in the here-and-now, influenced by the anterior cingulate cortex, and gets stuck in loops, preventing the brain from producing more effective self-regulation needed to resolve issues.

- Evidence suggests that epigenetic factors play an important role in development. For example, children of Holocaust survivors and children of famine survivors exhibit varied effects of traumatic experiences, suggesting that trauma suffered by parents and earlier generations may be passed along genetically, not by changes in the DNA itself, but by inherited changes in *how* DNA gets expressed. For trauma, many of the changes relate to stress-regulation and resilience-related genes. (Dias and Kessler 2014) and even within one lifetime (Yehuda et al. 2013). However, psychotherapy has been shown to reverse epigenetic changes in stress vulnerability related to trauma (Vinkers et al. 2019).

Taken together, these factors create a brain environment primed to attract and be attracted to others who are likely to trigger unresolved issues from the past (Buechler 2019; Johnson 2013). Without intervention, this is a recipe for repeated episodes of attraction and painful disappointment between parties who never really connect. However, if addressed effectively, this cycle presents the parties with opportunity to unlock brainlock and learn how to grow together. The authors call this process "re-association," or, more informally, "rupture and repair."

Interpersonal

Perhaps the most profound irony of brainlock is that it protects us from what we tell ourselves we're looking for in relationships: intimacy, empathy, emotional investment, and even vulnerability. Down deep, we may realize that these are characteristics of a mature relationship, but the prospect of allowing another person to become important in our lives is too scary to let it actually happen.

The neural networks affected by traumatic experience change the way we perceive and interpret others. For example, the anxious face of a loved one may be interpreted as the angry face of a punishing parent. Offers of help may be perceived as bids to manipulate and control. Conversely, I may view an exploitative person, or someone who offers care but never shows up, as someone I can depend on. The nature of the irrelationship dynamic is such that attempting to explore such miscommunication increases its likelihood or makes its participants dig their heels in further. The net result is that we're even less able to recognize genuine concern in others and more likely to gravitate toward the inauthenticity of irrelationship, simply because it's familiar.

Social-Contextual

Irrelationship is born out of the delusion that an unsafe world can be made safe through proper management. A small child not only doesn't understand emotions, but she believes that everything in the world has something to do with her. Therefore, she has no means of grasping that something going on in her caregiver's life—i.e., negative emotions—is the cause of the caregiver's emotional distance. As a result, the child blames this emotional distancing on the only available object: herself. She then uses a song-and-dance routine to try to fix whatever is wrong between herself and her caregiver so she can feel safe again. If the routine doesn't fix what's wrong with her caregiver, she will ultimately dissociate her anxiety, thus losing awareness of her own feelings of unsafety.

STAYING ON TARGET

Many of us can look back at our childhood years and identify events that drove us into the compulsive caretaking routines that resulted in brainlock. The following exercise examines such events and influences, the patterns that developed as a result, and how they created brainlock.

Exploring Song-and-Dance Routines and How They Play Out Now

The table below lists examples of anxiety-driven behaviors that you may have seen in your family—who performed them and how they affected your own behavior. For each example, read from left to right to gain insight into the underlying dynamics and purpose of each behavior.

Relationship patterns and behavior modeled for me	Who performed these behaviors	How these behaviors led to irrelationship patterns in myself
My mother and father obsessively criticized each other's behavior. At the same time, they often made a point of telling me how fortunate I was to be living with two parents.	My parents.	I often catch myself obsessing on others' "negative" behavior and use the behavior as either a) an excuse to keep my distance from them, or b) an opportunity to fix them, while c) viewing their behavior as proof that they have nothing useful to offer me.
My mother continually complained to my siblings and me about our father, but never spoke to him directly about her issues and feelings.	My mother.	I'm unable to address my issues with others' behavior, even when it negatively affects me. However, I always listen to their complaints about others, using those complaints as an excuse for devaluing and avoiding them.
My older siblings worried about our family finances, and as they grew older, sometimes confronted our parents about their spending. After each such confrontation, our parents went on spending binges.	Brother and sister.	I never question the behavior of people I'm close to. Instead, I go behind their backs trying to fix whatever problems they cause. This avoids embarrassment but has also left me unable to ask others for help when I need it.

With the table above as a guide, analyze behaviors in your own life:

- What connections can you make between behaviors you observed in your family growing up and your own behaviors today?

- What indications do you see that these behaviors you learned in your family may not be under your control now?

- What components of brainlock do you think may be active in your functioning today, and what do they look like? How do those behaviors help you? How do they interfere with how you would like to live?

- Being as specific as you can, describe feelings of ambivalence or disagreement you remember having *within yourself* when you had to make a choice about how to act in a particular situation. Describe the outcome of the choice you made, and the feelings you had as a result, positive and negative.

CHAPTER THREE

Performer and Audience

Through the Fourth Wall

Vito started his therapy session with a dream that had shaken him up. "I dreamed that I stumbled on a door that led into another dimension. But I refused to go through it."

In theater, the "fourth wall" is an invisible boundary between Performers and Audience, or in literature, between author and reader. At times, characters in plays break the fourth wall and speak directly to the Audience about something that's unfolding on the stage. The device was used often by Shakespeare, as well as in classical Greek theater

In irrelationship, we live with and enforce a fourth wall between ourselves and others. This psychological boundary keeps us in the same "production" without our coming too close to or speaking directly with each other—even, in some cases, when we're telling ourselves we want intimacy with others.

In the craziness of self-irrelationship, the vigilant boundaries that we erect and maintain between ourselves and others become inner barriers that keep us from engaging or even acknowledging different "currents" within ourselves. We enact internally misleading dialogues to convince ourselves we're doing everything we can to meet our interpersonal needs, when in fact we're enacting a compulsive caregiving routine upon ourselves that ensures such needs will remain unsatisfied. Our delusion of self-sufficiency cuts us off from our emotions, important memories, and genuine experiences of the world, usually resulting in our misinterpreting what's actually happening around us.

"I'd basically been a fly on the wall in the life of my family for years. I was always just a spectator."

Vito married in his late teens and was a father by the time he was twenty. The marriage ended before he turned twenty-four, leaving him with disappointment and infrequent contact with his son. In his early thirties, he met his second wife, Ruth. Her first marriage was similarly short-lived, and her two school-aged sons were more than happy to act as if they welcomed Vito into their lives.

"Somehow, I've always managed to keep out of center stage all my life," Vito elaborated.

The theatrical fourth wall allows the Audience to observe but not actively participate. In some types of literature, the fourth wall is used differently. The wisecracking Marvel Comics character Deadpool almost constantly breaks the fourth wall by addressing the reader directly. Similarly, in Kurt Vonnegut's *Breakfast of Champions*, the character Kilgore Trout breaks the fourth wall to beg Vonnegut to "Make me young!" More subtly, *Saturday Night Live*'s "Debbie Downer" (Rachel Dratch) looks straight into the camera and suppresses her laughter as the trombone blows, "Whaa-Whaahh!" Those acting out irrelationship, however, not only don't break, but don't acknowledge the fourth wall. Instead, they spare no energy to enforce a fictitious life that scrupulously avoids acknowledgment of their own genuine feelings or needs.

Despite some initial ambivalence in Ruth's children, due to their having been abandoned by their father, they came to love Vito and worked at welcoming him into their family life. Vito, however, persisted in unconsciously keeping himself at the edge of the life of his new family, despite how attractive it was to him. Vito described his childhood as "just fine." But upon a deeper analysis, it turned out that, as the only child of two "totally self-absorbed" parents, he thought that he had learned to "push down (his) need to be important to other people." His parents were especially unavailable emotionally for him as their marriage fell apart, thus convincing him that he must accept quietly whatever scraps he received from what was left of their family. But still, somehow he felt that if he'd been better able to convince them that he was "okay," and that he didn't need or want anything from them, their family would have been saved. Positioned as Audience, he revealed his investment in irrelationship, that is, as only a minor character in someone else's self-estranged existence. This kept him safely insulated in his self-constructed role on the periphery of family life. Similarly, because of the disappointment of her first marriage, Ruth and her sons were wary of trusting themselves to Vito initially, but their growing affection for him succeeded in penetrating this barrier.

In traditional psychoanalysis, the analyst assumes a mostly silent role in the therapeutic process. However, Vito's non-traditional analyst regularly broke the fourth wall, which encouraged Vito to take the same approach to his own life. "My job," his analyst said, "is to move you toward a conversation with parts of Vito that you either have trouble hearing or don't want to know about. The goal is for you to reappropriate pieces of your life you've been missing out on by staying at the fringes."

Poised at the boundary between inner and outer lives, Vito and his therapist began jointly pushing the boundaries of what was okay and not okay to talk about. At first, Vito was slow to access important feelings. Loneliness and longing were pretty easy for him to recognize, but the fear of owning his grief and shame was more complicated. These were at the bottom of his feeling unlovable and incompetent—feelings he'd carried since, as a teen, he'd been unable to save his mother and father's marriage. For Vito, anything was preferable to admitting to such a major "shortcoming."

By attacking his resistance directly, Vito and his therapist began undermining the fourth wall around the forbidden territory of Vito's inner life. This had the unexpected effect of softening Vito's resistance to allowing himself to be vulnerable with his new family.

"Letting myself reach out to Ruth's boys was huge. I wouldn't ever have believed I could have a life that was so different from what I was used to—that hole I'd been living in," Vito reflected. "Just being nice to myself instead of my constantly blaming myself for anything that didn't 'turn out right' made me able to figure out what I *really* felt about things—even stuff that isn't even personal."

"Well," his therapist replied, "like that awful old saying from the '70s goes, it sounds like you've started to 'find yourself.'"

Milestones for Song-and-Dance Development: Plurality within Singularity

In childhood, both the Performer and the Audience feel unsafe when they observe negative emotions in their caregiver. The Performer becomes the caregiver's caretaker until she or he is able to give care to the child, while the Audience takes an apparently passive role by pretending the care she's receiving is "adequate." This allows the caregiver to feel better about her- or himself. Both share the fear that they will never be "okay" without the rightly managed intervention. As stated earlier, if this pattern is carried into adulthood, genuine connection with others is all but impossible.

In self-irrelationship, this pattern is internalized, but with key differences. We act out the same kinds of song-and-dance routines, but as a response to how unsafe we feel *within ourselves*. For example, when upset with yourself, how do you treat yourself? Are you mercilessly self-critical? Do you reduce all your feelings into a narrow range of emotions, such as anger, confusion, or hopelessness, without trying to figure out what's actually happening within yourself? Perhaps you completely avoid thinking about what you want or need in a given situation, and instead "yell at yourself" for being "needy," thus feeding unconscious feelings of neglect and resentment.

These are types of experiences of our own crazy that, if they remain unaddressed, isolate us *from ourselves*, so that we have no way to figure out anything about parts of ourselves that are real.

Learning to balance various parts of ourselves while maintaining self-awareness and self-continuity is the healing process that puts our crazy to work for us.

Integration

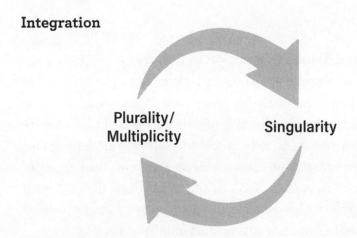

Plurality/Multiplicity   Singularity

In self-irrelationship, the Performer or Audience becomes a *self* that represents the sum total of techniques one uses to protect oneself from being overwhelmed by insecurity and anxiety. This is the conscious self-experience that defends against the anxiety resulting from past trauma that has been made inaccessible to consciousness (dissociated) and enacted in a compulsive caretaking role. This self-as-psychological-defense engages with an *other* (person) at one or more of the following levels:

- An actually occurring experience of another person.

- A fantasized experience of another person who poses the "threat" (or promise) of actual engagement with me.

- A flashback to a previous experience of another person that triggers irrelationship defenses, thus setting off my song-and-dance routine.

- My putting one of the different GRAFTS behavioral routines into play *within myself:* Good, Right, Absent, Funny, Tense, or Smart.

I may act out different roles with different people, depending on their role in my life and what they trigger. So you may sometimes act out as Performer, sometimes as Audience, but in either case, in order to reduce anxiety.

The Song-and-Dance in Relation to Others

Sometimes the rewards of a song-and-dance are so seductive that getting out of it is a hard sell. It's pretty heady for a performer to be complimented on knowing what someone else feels or needs before they know themselves, or to be praised for always doing things for others to make sure they're comfortable and "happy." The flip side of this is that such caretakers aren't driven by altruism, but by a need to appear to be a selfless good guy. It's even more confusing if actual caring is mixed in with the drive to meet one's own needs.

Similarly, who wouldn't find it exciting to meet a potential partner who "really understands me," and is "always putting himself out to make sure I'm comfortable? Only, it does get kind of tiresome that he always delivers his 'helpfulness' with well-intentioned analysis and advice about my faults and needs."

This pattern often develops in couples who rush into exciting new relationships without actually getting to know one another. Usually they're driven by an idealized fantasy they hope will make up for caregiving they missed when they were growing up. Or by adolescent ideas of what true love looks like. The magic we tell ourselves (usually repeatedly) eliminates the need to worry about being disappointed, betrayed, or abandoned—again.

When it finally dawns on me that "I've done it again," and "once again, got what I always got," that's the moment I can choose, without harshness or judgment, to start seeing my crazy and calling it by its real name. In other words, that's when I can start to get well.

Song-and-Dance Routine Interrupted

The following equation uses the roles, characteristics, and outcomes of irrelationship to help the reader "locate" him or herself in their song-and-dance routine. However, in the case of self-irrelationship, the implied "we" in the schema is actually parts of "me."

The PERFORMER
Gives until it hurts

Characteristics
Driven by anxiety; builds resentment and creates relational imbalance such as feelings of superiority, isolation, and false safety.

— plus—

AUDIENCE
Takes until it hurts

Characteristics
Driven by anxiety; impenetrability; pretends caretaking received is helpful, but actually sabotages the caretaker's caretaking by pretending to be fixed, helped, or cured.

— equals —

Neither Party Gives
(anxiety remains and includes devaluing of the other) and

Neither Party Receives
(anxiety remains while not allowing
either party to give to the other)

— equals —

Chronic emotional distance or absence.

Protection from awareness of anxiety and
vulnerability related to emotional investment.

— result —

Dissociation, Isolation, Depression,
i.e., IRRELATIONSHIP

STAYING ON TARGET

Exercise
Self-Irrelationship
THE "PERFORMER-ME"

1. What types of self-care do you practice and what are their goals? Do you have to force yourself to do these care activities, or do you find it easy to incorporate them into your routine? How do you feel when you do them? When you don't do them?

2. If you backslide from taking care of yourself, what do you do to get yourself back on track? What kinds of feelings are involved in this process?

3. Think of learning self-care as a process. What would it be like to be easy on yourself when you "fall short" of desired routines?

4. When you hear the expression "compassion on yourself," what comes to mind? How do you think compassion for yourself would affect your ability to achieve the goals you set?

5. Compare the previous question with the idea of self-discipline. What connection or disconnect do you see between compassion for yourself and self-discipline?

6. What feelings come up for you when you are, and are not, successful in taking care of yourself?

THE "AUDIENCE-ME"

1. What is it like for you to be alone with yourself at home? What feelings can you identify that come up at such times? What do you do either to prevent or to promote quiet time with yourself?

2. What do you think would happen if you tried making a practice of "turning everything off" when you come home from your daily routine and simply go about your regular activities in the quiet? What things would go through your head, positive and negative? How would you be likely to respond to those things?

3. Regarding the idea of self-compassion mentioned above, how could that fit in with the idea of being quiet when alone with yourself?

4. When you find yourself directing negative thoughts and criticism at yourself, what would it be like to put those thoughts on pause and try to figure out where they're coming from?

5. Has anyone ever told you that you were a perfectionist, or at any rate, over-demanding on them? If so, how did you react, both outwardly and inwardly?

Fears of Compassion Scales

Research supports the commonsense idea that fears hold us back from doing many things that may be good for us. Compassion is no exception. Identifying what the barriers to compassion are for oneself and others gives powerful, actionable information for building the capacity for health, self-love, and positive relationships, information about ourselves that is critical to know. Understanding fears allows us to square off with them and press forward to a better place.

We encourage you to visit https://www.compassionatemind.co.uk/resource/scales and download the Fears of Compassion scales developed by Professor Paul Gilbert and colleagues. These scales will help to measure your thoughts and beliefs regarding kindness and compassion in three areas of your life: 1) Expressing compassion for others, 2) Responding to compassion from others, and 3) Expressing kindness and compassion toward yourself.

PERFORMER *AND* AUDIENCE

Mutual relationships are unknown territory for many of us. Insight into the Performer/Audience dynamic can be used to create a space for safely considering your relationship with your own history and using that history as a tool for making your crazy work for you. The following exercise will be useful for gaining such insight.

Exercise

You as Performer

As an adult, the Performer presents as a do-gooder or rescuer whose compulsive song-and-dance routine often includes one or more of the following:

- Attempts to change the caregiver.

- Attempts to change oneself.

- Lets the caregiver off the hook for poor caretaking—usually by avoidance; may blame self for the caregiver's negative feelings.

- Ignores key personal or interpersonal issues and rejects anyone calling attention to them.

The following questions can help you decide if you fit the Performer role.

1. Do you find yourself doing for others because no one else will? What kinds of things?

2. Are you the one who always seems to be picking up the slack in your relationships, your household, or where you work? Give examples.

3. Does doing for others sometimes leave you with negative feelings about yourself or others? Give examples.

4. Do you sometimes get angry because things you do for others aren't appreciated or reciprocated appropriately? What have you done about feeling unappreciated?

5. When your partner seems unhappy, how do you respond? Is your response "real," or do you tailor it to what you believe it "should" be?

6. What feelings and behaviors do you observe in your life today that you connect with feelings and events from your childhood? Be specific.

7. Do you remember times when, as a child, a parent expected you to be a problem-solver or caregiver for others around you? Describe the incident(s) and how you think you were affected.

8. What kinds of things do you do to make sure your good qualities are recognized?

9. Have you ever had to leave a relationship because you disagreed or were uncomfortable with something going on in the relationship? Describe the incident.

10. Have you had the experience of romantic relationships that developed quickly and then ended suddenly? What happened and why?

Exercise

You as Audience

Performers unconsciously look for an Audience whose vulnerability would be a good fit with their own song-and-dance routine—all without disclosing the Performer's own vulnerability and needs.

The following questions can help you analyze whether you fit the Audience role.

1. Looking back at your childhood, do you remember a caregiver doing things "for you" that you didn't want or need? Do you remember being afraid to ask for something you needed because you were afraid of rocking the boat?

2. Do you expect your intimate partner to be a good caretaker? Have you been in relationships that failed because you didn't get the care you needed? What happened?

3. What happens when those around you see you becoming disturbed or unhappy? Do you have a fear of being abandoned if you show negative emotions?

4. Have you had the experience of a romantic partner "going overboard" in taking care of you? How did it feel, and what happened to that relationship?

5. When you start a new relationship of any kind, do you expect it to end disappointingly? How do you prepare yourself for that outcome?

6. What behaviors do you recognize in yourself as carryovers from your childhood?

7. Do you remember acting as if your parents were good parents even when they weren't, so that you didn't rock the boat? Do you sometimes let others believe they're right, so you don't lose the relationship? Give examples.

8. Do you sometimes act as if your partner is good at taking care of you when they aren't? Can you describe?

9. Does care and attention you receive from others sometimes make you feel uneasy or uncomfortable? Describe such a situation.

10. In your relationships, have you felt that your partner takes your decision-making out of your hands? How? What was going on and how did you respond?

11. Have you ever felt that the care given by someone close to you isolates you from others? What feelings has that created in you?

CHAPTER FOUR

The GRAFTS Behaviors: How Childhood Experiences Keep Us Crazy

The idea of self-irrelationship may sound *really* crazy because it involves thinking about *oneself* as made up of discrete parts with different ways of relating to one other. But theory around irrelationship-based relationships with others translates easily into the dynamics within an individual's psyche. For example, in self-irrelationship, the idea of *Audience* may take on several meanings simultaneously:

1. Conscious beliefs and behaviors designed to make me *think* that I'm looking after myself "properly," although I still have feelings that seem connected with trauma, being neglected, or being authentically cared for while continuing to experience negative feelings that seem to match an experience of trauma, anxiety, neglect, doubt, and fear—feelings that I associate (perhaps dimly) with my childhood.

2. Acting as if the caretaking I'm giving myself is responsible and effective while simultaneously being haunted by the belief that I'm neglected and don't always show up for myself the way I should.

3. I intervene on my own behalf so I can feel safe while simultaneously pretending that being alone doesn't make me uneasy.

4. At times, I make a point of stepping back so I can deliberately scrutinize my feelings, thoughts, and experiences, including past traumas.

In the case of 4, while the Audience may have dissociated from a disturbing experience, he's also able to transform it by witnessing it in real time, thereby relating *internally* to what is happening with the Performer. Over time, such purposeful connection with our experience can change my sense of my own identity: Trauma resolves into sadness, wisdom, acceptance, and even gratitude. Old wounds leave scars, but heal nevertheless.

If we don't choose such acceptance of our experience, negative consequences will mount over time, leading, for example, to deterioration of self-care, substance abuse, and disruption of personal growth as well as damage to personal and professional relationships.

Self-irrelationship may include more than one Performer and more than one Audience. In fact, many people identify with two or three coherent modes of interaction with the world. For example, we may, at times, convey an image of kindness and patience, while at other times we feel impatient and irritable. Periods of optimism and resilience may alternate with periods of depression that match others' expectations. Sometimes it may even seem as if somebody flipped a switch that brought out one or the other. That "switch" could be the anniversary of a traumatic event, the birthday of an abuser, or the approach of holidays. Sometimes the effect is so severe that people report difficulty remembering what it was like to feel good or just "normal" and doubt that they'll ever feel good again.

This dichotomy of narcissistic cores fits with Performer-Audience model; i.e., Nice/Mean, Happy/Depressed, etc. The most obvious cases may be accompanied by clear, if not vocal, parts of oneself, such as the silent "inner child," or the adult spectator of others' experiences, positive or negative. We may act out these different parts of ourselves only in very safe or very risky situations or contexts, such as during a trip to a favorite place, or when sexually aroused.

In this sense, we come to fill a role for ourselves similar to that which Bromberg describes for the therapist treating the fragmented patient:

[The analyst] is often in a hypnoid state qualitatively similar to that which his patient is in, and sometimes becomes fixated, concretely, upon the verbal content of the session; the words begin to take on an "unreal" quality, and this is frequently what "wakes the analyst up" to the fact that something is "going on." He has been hypnoidally dissociated from that part of himself that was participating in the enactment, but once he regains access to it, he will no longer be "asleep" to the fact that the patient, although using words, is equally "asleep" to the here-and-now experience between them.[1]

Working through self-irrelationship will take interaction with another person (not necessarily a therapist) that includes naming one's dissociated parts. This may look crazy, but is, in fact, an active part of reassociating dissociated states and experiences.

Attachment Style and Self–Other Experience

Some high-functioning people appear to be emotionally sturdy, coherent, and fully integrated, concealing what psychoanalysts call an *insecure attachment style*. This lockdown of oneself limits self-perception, access to others, and the potential for close relationships. Such denial of oneself is, as explained above, a survival tool by which we divert our attention from developmental trauma and dissociation of it. Common markers of it are the inability to remember significant childhood events; ability to recall heightened emotional states such as joy or fear; or recalling "flashes" of past experiences that don't fit together into an intelligible storyline. This dovetails with persons with insecure attachment style, who recall only fragments of difficult experiences. Their accounts of such experiences are often full of pauses, changes in direction, skipping around, bizarre word choices, and confusion of verb tenses such as "she is" rather than "she was" when describing events from the past. Such narratives correlate with unresolved trauma, grief, dissociation, and dysfunction in personal relationships. On the other hand, autobiographical accounts by well-integrated individuals are frank about missing pieces while presenting a narrative whole that reveals self- awareness, comprehension, and a willingness to use history to improve self-understanding.

Interplay between two people with insecure attachment style is likely to snowball rapidly into a crisis. For example, if an adult who typically avoids intimacy becomes preoccupied with a potential but avoidant partner, the avoidant person will increasingly retreat from the connection, provoking an anxiety-driven pursuit by the preoccupied person, often with a dramatic and unpleasant resolution. Similarly, in those invested in self-irrelationship, narcissism clashes with harsh self-criticism and blocks self-awareness. For example, I may agree to do something I don't want to do. When the time comes, I go through with it, making me feel angry and ashamed. But if I start to accept and listen to my interior conflicts I can turn them into something satisfying and even pleasant. *That's* letting my crazy work for me.

On the other hand, blocking consciousness of conflicting emotions can lead to intolerance of *any* frank emotional experience, negative or positive, including distancing myself from anyone I'm attracted to, or who's attracted to me. Does this mean the person in self-irrelationship will never be able to connect with others? Attachment theory and our clinical experience indicate otherwise. "Earned secure attachment"[2] can be created if we allow compassionate empathy *for ourselves* to look frankly at the childhood experiences that made us create the song-and-dance routines that ensure that those around us are kept at a safe distance.

Managing all these moving parts can be so confusing that I'm tempted to go back into my song-and-dance hiding place. However, even just a modicum of willingness to accept and to take care of myself can be enough to blast open the parts of me that prevent my participation in real life.

Exercise
Reflecting on Your Own Family
Does irrelationship live in your family history? The following simple exercise may provide clues.

- Write down the names of people who were important to you when you were a small child. It can be anyone from a family member to a virtual stranger with whom you had a memorable encounter. Write reflections or even single-word impressions you have about each person that relate to how you view that person now.

- What connections do you see between how they treated you and how you behave toward others now?

GRAFTS: Types of Song-and-Dance Routines
Our song-and-dance routines are techniques we developed as small children to help our caregivers to help us. Over time, these techniques taught us to organize the world according to: 1) My need to be a caregiver; and 2) My demand that people around me play their part in the routine.

What do these routines look like in a child?

A variety of interactive patterns (the authors use the acronym, "GRAFTS" as shown in the table that follows) become grafted onto a child's personality in response to her or his experience with early caregivers. The following table includes brief descriptions of each GRAFTS behavior and why the child starts using it.

	Descriptors	Explanation
G	Good	We believe our caregiver needs us to be a "good" girl or boy, driving us to be good all the time with everybody.
R	Right	We're driven to do everything exactly right, hoping, and finally believing, that doing so will make our caregiver feel better. Sometimes this develops into a need to be strong or competent in all situations.
A	Absent	We believe we can help our caregivers by staying out of their way. This is often seen in children of a severely depressed parent, but sometimes in children whose parents are not engaged or who have poor coping skills. The Absent routine is virtually always characteristic of the Audience.
F	Funny	The child is constantly "on," looking for ways to make the caregiver laugh, thus dispelling their negative emotions.
T	Tense	This adaptation is a constant state of unconscious anxiety that keeps us walking on eggshells so that we don't upset our caregiver. We also avoid thinking about or calling attention to our own needs.
S	Smart	In households where intelligence is valued, children elicit attention by making themselves knowledgeable in areas calculated to please the caregiver. Children locked in this behavior often deprive themselves of exploring their own interests.

Once we figure out which GRAFTS behavior is the most effective mood changer, we make it our "first line of defense" against anxiety. Thus we learn to believe in our ability to fix our caregivers by changing their mood, which then makes us feel safer.

Off the Edge of the Earth

"My mother frequently told me," Julian recalled in therapy, "that she never wanted to have me. Pretty much every time we got into an argument, which was often, she'd throw in my face that the only reason she had me and my sister was because our father threatened to divorce her."

Some childhood environments are so inhospitable, and even hateful, that the only way to be in a caretaking role is to disappear. To feel unwelcome in our families is to live in relentless trauma. In such a state, our character develops around a kernel of endlessly assaulted self which must be protected at all costs. The song-and-dance routine developed in this brutal environment performs its caretaking by the most extreme, and possibly only, available means: complete absence.

"I've survived two decades of believing that I'm HIV-positive. I've always told myself that that was why I couldn't date anybody, or even let anybody get close to me. Well, since I've never really done anything that could give me HIV, I guess I've been telling myself I'm positive all these years for some other reason."

The mind is highly resourceful at finding ways to keep us alive. Growing up in a poisonous cloud of pain and fear may require a complete shutdown for the individual to make it out alive. Song-and-dance routines shut down *awareness* of unbearable fear and pain, though the feelings themselves aren't eliminated. But song-and-dance routines are markers of those split-off feelings. Short of suicide, emotional disappearance from one's own life is probably the most severe available routine possible for the social human creature.

When irrelationship song-and-dance routines take the form of obsessive-compulsive routines (as often happens), they dovetail with the individual's chosen GRAFTS behavior. This can be seen in how Julian obsessively used his supposed HIV infection to maintain Absence and total isolation—a technique he originally deployed against his mother's assaultiveness and his father's default into silence.

Though at first Julian almost violently rejected his therapist's questioning the "HIV defense," he gradually became willing (after repeatedly canceling his therapy appointments) to reframe it as an excuse for keeping others away—including his therapist. "Our starting place and first goal in doing therapy," his therapist explained, "is for us to get you out of the place you've been hiding. We do that by taking a hard look at what happens between you and me in this office, and yes, every time you call me to tell me you're not coming, or not coming back *ever*. That's how we piece together the how and why of your disappearing self. And that's how the cure starts."

STAYING ON TARGET

The GRAFTS Assessment

Spotting GRAFTS behaviors in others is usually easier than picking up on them in yourself. This is partly because, while GRAFTS behaviors are self-defeating, they can also look and feel like self-care. But the reality is that GRAFTS behavior within oneself includes a subtext of harsh and punishing self-talk that's the opposite of caring and acceptance. At the same time, naming the discomfort and anger behind our GRAFTS behavior is vital to not torpedoing the process of moving beyond them.

The following exercise will help you to identify GRAFTS behaviors you've used and why. Write two lists: One, of GRAFTS behaviors you see in your family and in other relationships, and one of GRAFTS you've used, or may be using, in/on yourself. After completing the lists, examine each behavior, using the bullet points below as a guide. Keep in mind that we sometimes use different GRAFTS at different times, and may even use more than one simultaneously.

- What childhood GRAFTS behaviors did you continue to use as you grew older? Did they change as you got older? Did any of them disappear?

- Who did you target with your GRAFTS behaviors as a child and now? How did they respond?

- We may use GRAFTS in a variety of situations:
  » in the workplace.

  » with friends.

  » with family members.

  » in romantic or potentially romantic situations.

Thinking of specific situations in which you've used a GRAFTS, what triggered it? When triggered, were you aware of consciously deciding to use it? Are you able to see yourself using it as it's occurring, or are you not aware of it at all?

- How do you think using GRAFTS behaviors affects your social life? Work life? Finances? Physical health? State of mind?

- What feelings or events you've experienced in a current relationship (any type of relationship) had a role in your deciding to explore irrelationship and GRAFTS? Describe what happened.

Exercise
GRAFTS Role Reversal
Each item in the GRAFTS table that follows represents a role reversal in which a child takes on a caretaking role for the caregiver. Such flipping of roles and boundaries has a big impact on how safe the child feels.

In this exercise, reading left to right, see if you can relate to the examples of GRAFTS behavior in the two examples in the table. Then come up with your own examples of ways that your own behavior impacts how you connect or don't connect with others.

Role Reversal	Who I Was Performing For	Impact on Me
My mother was always criticizing and comparing herself to other mothers, so I worked harder at school so she'd be proud of me and not so hard on herself.	My mother.	I ended up acting like a "know-it-all" at school as well as at home, which annoyed other kids and made them avoid me.
My parents fought a lot, so I learned to distract them by pretending to do a musical or comedy routine on an imaginary stage.	My parents.	I took over responsibility for my mom and dad's relationship, and for anything else that went wrong in our home. Though sometimes they got mad at me for not minding my own business.

Exercise
Using GRAFTS Routines on Myself
Review the GRAFTS exercises you've already completed, identifying ways that you used GRAFTS when you were growing up. Then, with the examples in the following table as a guide, try to figure out how your GRAFTS routines got started, and how you use them in your relationships now.

Roles I Play	How and Where My Role Originated	Effects of My Role on Me
Playing the victim.	It was how my father reacted to my mother's domineering behavior in order to keep the peace.	I avoid thinking about my real needs so that I don't put demands on others, or become resentful about past unmet needs or losses.
I stay silent when anything goes wrong in my relationship with my boyfriend.	When I was a kid, my family lived with my father's parents, who constantly criticized my mom. My father never stood up for her.	I keep my mouth shut when something happens that I don't like. Later, I get mad at myself for not saying anything, and punish myself by lashing out at friends to alienate myself from them.

PART II

TREATING YOUR CRAZY

CHAPTER FIVE

Compassionate Empathy

Jumping through Hoops

"It was Father's Day," Chris began, "and Maya and I were so wrecked from our daughter's sleepover party that we started sniping at each other."

Chris and Maya had been in couples therapy for a little over a year, trying to get to the bottom of how irrelationship works within oneself.

"We've learned enough to know when danger's approaching and hit the pause button so we can both take a moment to remember how much we actually care about each other," Maya put in. "But, well, sometimes we see what's coming and hit pause faster than other times. So in the morning, we went out for coffee like we always do Sunday mornings. But that Sunday was . . ."

"Father's Day," Chris put in. "And all I *really* wanted to do was to hang out at home and celebrate being a father to your—to our—kids."

"Only, I had different ideas. A *lot* of different ideas. It was partly because you've always done such nice things for me and for the kids on 'our' special days, so I wanted to do something really nice for you. So I made all these plans . . ."

"Yeah," sighed Chris, "in a way, we were falling for *my* old routine, even though you were the one doing the performing this time."

Chris (and Maya) had made a lot of progress toward not buying into Chris's old Performer song-and-dance routine, which sometimes made Maya tease Chris, calling him the family Activities Director. But on that Father's Day, the shoe was on the other foot.

"I just wasn't willing to let go of what *I* wanted to do for *you*. And," she paused. "It was a disaster."

Maya and Chris had both made a lot of progress identifying and working through their individual self-irrelationship-based strongholds—the self-imposed lockdowns that stood in the way of their being able to accept self-care (compassionate empathy), even for themselves.

"We'd already learned a lot about how much we 'needed' our self-isolation routines." Chris paused to chuckle. "They were even going strong the day we got married. Well, as things moved on, and Maya got more and more into the role of 'stay-at-home' wife and mother, I just stepped back and played the Audience, hiding behind my do-gooding on weekends and holidays, while my Maya drove herself nuts 'looking after' me and our daughters. The really bizarre takeaway of all this for me (when I finally let myself see it) was that letting things go along like that was how I avoided thinking about how scary it was to be so vulnerable to this person I'm totally crazy about. I've never let *anybody* mean so much to me!"

"Of course," added Maya, "all those plans I made weren't *all* about doing something special for Chris. It was really *my* thing, *my* project, just like the little projects my mother gave me when I was little. I had almost no friends, and my poor mom just didn't know what to do about it. So she'd think up stuff for me to do to keep me busy. And sometimes it really wasn't appropriate. I remember one time she even made me do all the decoration and setting-up for my birthday party—a party that nobody came to except her, my father, and my brother. It was so strange, so—I don't know what it was. But it was so sad—*I* was so sad, but I didn't dare let my mom see that. So I had to pretend it was the best birthday ever. And when I met Chris, his being afraid of how he loved me gave me plenty of room to knock myself out doing all that stuff for him—only it was really for *me*. It was me and my mother all over again."

Compassionate empathy allows us to imagine and experience what others experience as they go down a path that we're familiar with. It then becomes a tool for reassociating parts of ourselves that were split off in early childhood. The example of Chris and Maya shows how two people invested in self-irrelationship can continue their self-imposed song-and-dance routines *while together*. But when they catch themselves (and one another) in the act, they can use that bit of crazy to figure out the gap between their authentic and their pathological needs.

The pathological part leads us to taking on someone else's needs as if they were our own, without realizing that we're actually violating that person. But we have the choice of learning to slow down, take a look at what we're doing, and see it for what it is. Every time we practice doing that, we strike a blow against the dissociation within ourselves, which makes us able to make decisions in our interactions with others that respect their personhood and boundaries.

"We ended up having a great Father's Day after all. I knew enough about my own routine to know that I needed to jerk myself back and look at what Maya was doing—not so much to me, but to herself. Well, and to me too. Then, when I reflected that back to her, well . . ."

"Yeah, it's true," Maya interrupted, grinning. "I missed a beat—or two—at first, and then I saw the whole thing and just started laughing. And so did Chris. So then we started Father's Day all over again. And it turned out great. We started out by doing some of the things I'd planned, but ended up just doing whatever wherever we went. And it was wonderful. Just being together really was the best part, just like

Chris said he wanted! I can't wait to see what happens next month on my birthday!"

Loneliness and Co-Loneliness?

Loneliness while in the company of others is not only a symptom of self-irrelationship; it's a major trigger for an irrelationship connection with another person. But it's also a key indicator that I'm bottoming out on my song-and-dance routine, which makes it a golden opportunity to start allowing my crazy to work for me.

For those just beginning to discover how irrelationship affects their connections with others, exploring what lies behind their song-and-dance routine is frightening. What if you discover that, down deep, you and/or your partner really aren't all that into each other?

Fear of rejection can be real enough, but the backstory of those brainlocked in self-irrelationship is usually that the real fear is you'll wind up with someone who accepts you as you really are and isn't afraid to learn the bad things about you—in other words, wants intimacy with you.

Compassionate empathy is the practice of unconditional acceptance and caring for others and, in the care of self-irrelationship, for oneself—a prerequisite for accepting rather than diverting yourself and others from your real history, including your history of trauma. As a practice, it allows me to see the different parts of myself, to differentiate which behaviors are and are not useful; that is, a life free of the GRAFTS of song-and-dance routines.

Couples therapy for Chris and Maya entailed work on recovery from the trauma each had dissociated, which was blocking the self-awareness and acceptance that would allow them to risk loving and being loved by their partner "as is." A bonus is that the process also recovered awareness of the emotional connection that brought them together in the first place. Plus, by taking joint ownership of the positive and negative feelings acted out in their song-and-dance routine, each could own the anxiety that they had long suffered in isolation, making it a piece of the manageable crazy and of the intimacy they were now building.

Compassionate empathy, then, allows *both parties* to share what *both parties* bring to the table. Later in the book you will learn about our techniques for making such sharing part of the baseline functioning of your relationship.

The Co-Isolation Agreement Between Us and the World

Forty-eight years into their marriage, Rick and Maureen's relationship finally hit the wall the two had tacitly agreed to erect when Rick first came home from his deployment to Vietnam. The agreement consisted in Maureen's not asking Rick about Vietnam, while Rick never let on that he needed Maureen's emotional support, no matter how distressed the emotional impact of his war experiences made him feel.

"It was humiliating," Rick said in therapy, after acknowledging that he had broken the rule. "I was seventy-two years old, I couldn't sleep, and I couldn't get away from feeling ashamed and afraid. And I had no idea why.

"For all those years, Maureen and I had our own routines. We had it all figured out and organized who would do what to take care of the house and make sure each other and the children were okay. And it seemed to work for a long time. Looking back, I can see—I know—Maureen and I were never really 'connected.' She did what she did and I did what I did. It didn't seem strange; it was what marriage 'looked like' in those years. But I didn't like the feeling that Maureen didn't really know how I felt about *anything*."

Their older daughter was married about fifteen years to a man who, in later years, was determined to have severe narcissistic personality disorder traits. During a lengthy divorce, he went to extreme lengths to hurt his wife and their two adolescent children, apparently to punish them for no longer not accepting him as he had always been, i.e., self-absorbed and unable or unwilling to show love for his family.

Rick didn't know how to help his daughter and grandchildren and felt terrible about it. All he could think of to say was, "I can't just go and kill him."

But he couldn't stop thinking about it either. He developed insomnia driven by ruminations on shame and fear of "what might happen," without being able to specify to himself what exactly he meant by that.

Maureen, meanwhile, became frightened as she watched Rick become increasingly "moody and unlike himself." Finally her worry overcame her resistance to breaking their old, unspoken contract. She suggested that he call the psychologist at the VA Clinic he was required to see annually in order to maintain his veteran's benefits.

In the middle of all this, Rick had a dream in which an unidentified set of skills were being tested for some indeterminate secret mission. After repeated failures, he finally passed the test, but still felt a deep sense of failure, as if succeeding was itself a failure. Then, when on the secret mission, he rounded a corner, only to encounter himself as a young man dressed in his military uniform. The sight moved him to terror, disgust, and a desire to destroy that person—only he could not make himself do it.

In desperation, Rick told his psychologist about the dream, along with some of his experiences while in Vietnam fifty years earlier— experiences he'd never told anyone. One such episode was a secret reconnaissance mission into enemy territory. Another was a mission that included many other young men like himself, one that had been kept totally "off the books," never to be discussed or even referred to again. "I still see the faces of my friends—my friends who died, and I didn't," he said through tears. "I would do anything to get rid of this— to kill whatever or whoever—to get rid of what happened to—what I did and those guys who died. Are dead. And all I have is that I'm so ashamed I can't sleep. And if I fall asleep, I wake up sometimes after ten minutes, sometimes after sleeping hours, scared out of my mind for no reason I can figure out."

In his therapy Rick talked mostly about how he'd developed an apathy, even an antipathy, toward everybody around him. "In 'Nam, people around me—guys I cared about—were getting killed every day. I'd finally got to a place where it had to stop—I had to stop thinking about it because it was killing me slowly." This had the added "benefit" of shutting down his awareness of his fear. In other words, he'd turned himself into someone who's "just like my son-in-law," he finally brought out one day.

"When I came home from the war, I thought I'd left that guy behind, dead in some battle I couldn't remember. Oh yeah, I'd also started drinking in 'Nam. Drinking a lot. And I kept it up when I got home. But no matter whether I drink or not, I *still* want to kill my son-in-law—that little bastard who—who is just like what that goddamn war made me!" Rick had shut down his ability to care for others by not even giving himself space in his head to think about them, or, really, about everything that was happening around him. It had finally dawned on Rick that he needed to make a change when he realized he was coming to resemble his narcissistic son-in-law, hurting and pushing others away in the process of avoiding recognizing and dealing with his trauma and vulnerability.

At the suggestion of the VA therapist, Rick and Maureen began short-term couples therapy to help Maureen understand what Rick was going through. But what ended up happening was that when Rick finally was able to put into words the connection between his guilt, self-hatred, and the feelings about his son in law, he began to smash the barrier that had kept him isolated from Maureen and his daughters for forty-eight years. While Maureen's asking him to get help at the VA was a violation of their unspoken contract, Rick's realization of his own feelings helped him to appreciate the impossible task she'd been shouldering for most of their married life, and the risk she took by finally stepping outside of the barrier they'd consensually built between them. Fortunately, her gamble paid off. He was able to flip his own script, from long-term self-destruction to embracing the young man who'd suffered so badly in wartime operations.

In addition to the excitement of reopening himself to his love for Maureen, Rick's experience had another quite unlooked-for outcome. As his daughter was brought into confidence about what his wartime experience had done to her father, she came to yearn to reach out to her own husband, with whom she had after all spent fifteen years of her life. She caught him off guard one day by reaching out to him, with an outcome that, over time, became strangely similar to what had happened to her mother and father. In time, Rick discovered a deep kinship and affection for his son-in-law. But that's a story for another book.

Reflecting on it all, Rick remarked that "I thought I was helping my family by keeping my ugly history in the dark and not even thinking about it myself. The isolation Maureen and I unknowingly agreed on all those years before almost killed me—and maybe Maureen too."

"What really surprised me," Maureen added, "was figuring out how badly we missed each other without realizing it. That's what's been *really* hurtful all this time. I can't even tell you how happy I am to be back with the man I love."

STAYING ON TARGET

Is Dependency Bad?

Working through irrelationship and onto the path of relationship sanity involves uncovering and analyzing various types of dysfunctional dependency (we sometimes call them "counter-dependency") that have long been part of our lives. This can become confusing, however, as we learn to surrender to healthy dependency.

Following is a table of contrasting attitudes and behaviors associated with irrelationship and with the mechanisms of relationship sanity, which you will learn to use when practicing the 40-20-40, or Self–Other Assessment (as we've referred to it in our previous books for use in relationships with others), found later in this book.

	Counter-dependent Song-and-Dance Routines Resulting in Irrelationship	Compassionate Empathy as Process of Relationship Sanity
Thwarting vs. Receiving	• I don't allow others to help me because I'm afraid of what it will cost me. • I don't allow others to know about my needs. • I don't accept instruction or advice. • I hide things I don't like about myself.	• I'm receptive and responsive to help offered by others. • I seek and make use of support from others. • I don't need constant care and reassurance to feel okay. • I'm able to tell others when I feel anxious and insecure.
Unreliable vs. Dependable	• I have trouble staying with a task and following through on even small commitments • I avoid problems and conflicts by giving in to others' wishes even when they're contrary to my opinions, feelings, or needs.	• Reliability is important to me. I feel strongly about showing up—even for relatively small commitments. • I have a history of reliability and trustworthiness. • I believe it's important to persist at finding solutions to issues that satisfy all affected parties.

	Counter-dependent Song-and-Dance Routines Resulting in Irrelationship	Compassionate Empathy as Process of Relationship Sanity
Exemption vs. Accountability	• I look for ways to blame and find fault. • I hide and deny my questionable behavior. • I hide my mistakes or avoid taking responsibility for them. • I assume and don't shy away from telling others their problems are their own fault. When complex situations go wrong, I look for a scapegoat.	• I take responsibility when I'm at fault. • I accept accountability for my contributions to problems and conflicts, and make amends when I hurt others. • I can acknowledge parts of myself that aren't as mature as I'd like. • I make and keep commitments.
Fear of Isolation vs. Healthy Independence	• I don't like being alone, but I still feel isolated when I'm with others. • I have a hard time setting boundaries and feel hurt, confused, and frustrated when others' boundaries seem to exclude me. • I hesitate to put myself forward because I'm afraid of being ridiculed or rejected. • I don't have clear ideas about what I really think, believe, and care about. • I seek and worry about not getting attention and approval from others in pretty much every area of my life.	• I'm clear about needing to be alone at times and can enjoy it. • I'm able to set boundaries, accept those set by others, and believe this to be healthy. • My ideas, opinions, and feelings are entitled to respect even when others disagree with them. • I am interested in furthering my understanding of myself. • I am comfortable with who I am.

	Counter-dependent Song-and-Dance Routines Resulting in Irrelationship	Compassionate Empathy as Process of Relationship Sanity
Passive and/ or Aggressive vs. Assertive	• I'm aggressive with others as a means of getting my needs and desires met. • I avoid overt conflict but will do anything covertly to make sure I get my way. • I believe bullying others is acceptable to get what I want. • In conflict situations, I don't stand up for I think, want, or need. • I let others off the hook if they don't support and care for me in difficult times.	• I'm able to ask for what I need. • I do my part to ensure that my plans come to fruition. • I can engage in conflict directly in order to solve problems and resolve differences. • I like and am engaged in my life. • I can disclose and struggle with conflicting feelings and ideas to invite the support of others.
Disregard/ Disdain vs. Positive Regard	• Criticism and shaming others is sometimes necessary to get what I want. • I sometimes withhold opinions out of concern that others "wouldn't be able to take it." • I impose my will on others when I know what's best for them. • I believe devaluing myself and others is appropriate at times. • I believe it's often my place to fix, or rescue, others.	• I'm usually able to find ways to care for myself. • I seek and find ways to show care and respect for others. • I respect the right and need for others to find solutions to their problems, but will offer help if asked. • I respect the dignity and rights of others, regardless of their emotional, psychological, spiritual, and intellectual development. • I believe in offering nurture and care to others based on mutual respect and efficacy.

	Counter-dependent Song-and-Dance Routines Resulting in Irrelationship	Compassionate Empathy as Process of Relationship Sanity
Self-Sufficient vs. Partnership	• I avoid helping others and don't let them help me. • I am able to work things out on my own and believe others should do the same. • My solutions are mine, and I deserve credit for them. • I pride myself on being independent and self-sufficient. • I sometimes believe it's necessary to allow others to believe they're in charge, while I quietly find ways to undermine them and exercise power behind the scenes. • I have difficulty accepting gifts and compliments from others.	• I am willing to offer and accept help. • I am willing to offer assistance without taking charge. • Problem solving with others is gratifying and likely to create novel, more effective solutions. • I enjoy sharing management, ownership, and leadership. • I enjoy collaborating on and implementing others' projects. • I enjoy receiving compliments, and accept gifts with gratitude.

As you contemplate each of the habits listed in the table, make note of instances in which you believe you see them at work in your current relationships with romantic partners, friends, family, colleagues, whoever. As you write, refer back to the table as needed, but don't overthink; give the first answer that comes to mind.

Next, review your responses and recall a specific interaction that left you feeling dissatisfied, even if the interaction didn't include overt conflict. Look for concrete examples of how you think irrelationship behaviors left you feeling uncomfortable, resentful, isolated, angry, hurt, or afraid.

Exercise

From Self-Irrelationship to Compassionate Empathy

The table below contrasts irrelationship-based attitudes and behaviors with those of people who integrate compassionate empathy in their functioning. Remember to keep in mind that compassionate empathy is a *practice* rather than a *goal*.

	Self-Irrelationship	Compassionate Empathy
Isolation vs. Showing Up	· I keep my feelings to myself. · I avoid making myself available to others—usually because I'm afraid of what they'll think of me. · I keep my head down to avoid drawing attention to myself. · I have a hard time responding to others' needs. · I easily seem to get lost in my own head rather than being present to others.	· I can share my feelings when I believe others are interested in me. · I'm open to being available for others. · I can give and receive attention to and from others. · I'm gratified by responding to others' needs; I can communicate my desire for connection and reciprocation. · I enjoy being in company of others.

	Self-Irrelationship	Compassionate Empathy
Depletion vs. Creativity	• I prefer to let others take the initiative. • I tend toward solitude both at home and in my work life. • I feel wary, drained, and even ripped off when others want something from me. • When a situation forces me to reach out to others, I have to overcome embarrassment and shame to go through with it. • Most things that happen to me are outside my control.	• I am able and willing to ask for help from others. • I can enjoy both solitude and the company of others. • Sharing tasks and resources feels empowering and energizing. • I feel that others are willing to help me when I need it. • I can share my concerns and problems with others.
Avoidance vs. Accessibility	• I instigate conflict to prevent resolution of issues both inside and outside myself. • I avoid addressing relationship issues. • I avoid initiative or leadership roles, so that I can't get blamed if anything goes wrong. • My life seems largely to be made up of issues that never get resolved.	• I prefer going through conflict until resolution is reached and every party understands underlying issues. • I listen for my own part in conflict so I can own it and contribute to the solution. • I try to remember to reflect on my feelings before I take action to avoid muddying the waters. • I'm okay with not having the answers to relationship problems and get a lot out of working through them jointly. • I try to analyze complex problems and work through them sensibly in an orderly way.

	Self-Irrelationship	Compassionate Empathy
Unavailability vs. Openness	· I mostly keep my thoughts and feelings to myself. · I rarely seek advice on important decisions, or even mention them to others. · I avoid putting myself in a position where I might be asked to help others with their issues. · I maintain the appearance of being busy to discourage others from asking anything of me.	· I try to maintain openness to others' need for care and support. · I prefer to bounce important decisions off others whose judgment or experience I respect. · I share what's going on with me when I'm confused about a problem or relationship.
Resentment vs. Generosity	· Situations that seem to call for an empathic response from me make me uneasy. · Validating or complimenting others makes me afraid I'm exposing myself or giving away too much.	· I value empathetic exchange and value the support of others. · I can express appreciation for others in words and actions. · I find ways to give negative feedback to others without putting them down.

	Self-Irrelationship	Compassionate Empathy
Non-Acceptance vs. Acceptance	• My feelings of unease get in the way of my enjoying being with others and experiences they find pleasurable. • If I observe problems in situations or other people, I feel that I should step in and try to fix them even when it's annoying or inconvenient. • I avoid problem situations unless I can control the outcomes. • The prospect of change in relationships or life-situations frightens me.	• I'm able to use humor as a tool in addressing problems with others. • I accept that life isn't always to my liking, but can remove myself from harmful situations. • I'm open to new projects and adventures and seeing where they will take me. • Any life experience, positive or negative, has potential to impact my life positively.

As you contemplate the behaviors set out in the table,

- Make note of items you see in yourself.

- Make note of any that you can see in your life today—both in casual situations, and with people you feel have signaled to you a desire to know you better.

- Refer back to the table as needed, but don't overthink it. Write down your thoughts as they occur to you.

CHAPTER SIX

Becoming a Good
Self-Parent

Starter Kid

"It's okay, Daddy. It was scary, but it's okay now."

Sami had winced, closed her eyes, and put her head down as her father blew up at the security guard when asked for identification.

"Oh, gosh! Sami, I'm so sorry I made you see me do that! You know I'm trying to do better!"

Ken's apology was abashed and real, but it didn't stop Sami's flashback to a time when her father's outbursts were a recurring part of their family life—a part that he and Sami's mother, Marie, would almost immediately pretend wasn't happening. Over time, not dealing with those outbursts left Sami feeling less and less safe with both of her parents.

Many of us don't remember major traumatic events from childhood, or don't have the skills to make sense of them. Sami's parents left her on her own when it came to dealing with the effects of Ken's loss of control, and the only technique she had for doing so was to put them as far out of mind as she could. Ironically, such "adapting by distancing" makes it more likely that Sami will repeat her father's explosive pattern. Not acknowledging traumatic experience creates a "divide" in mind and personality—the quintessential setup for self-irrelationship.

Ken and Marie were thrilled to learn that Marie was pregnant with Sami ten months into the "honeymoon period" of their relationship, and two months before their wedding. However, their honeymoon came to an abrupt halt when Sami was eighteen months old. They were living in Ken's apartment, which had been fine for him as a bachelor; now they needed a larger space, but an adverse market left them stuck where they were. Then mounting debt, a baby who had learned to walk, and finally Marie's diagnosis with a serious medical condition formed a perfect storm of everyday real life that rapidly pushed them to an emotional breaking point. Though both Ken and Marie consciously tried to avoid blaming each other for the turns their lives had taken, each unconsciously harbored resentment against the other.

A serious reframing of their relationship was needed, but Ken and Marie's plates were so full that it didn't begin to happen before Sami's feelings of security had already been seriously disturbed. Accustomed to warm caregiving, Sami found herself in a strange place of ongoing anxiety once such care came to a halt, and she had to fend for herself. In classic irrelationship form, she took on a caretaking role toward her mother and father by asking, telling, or begging them not to fight, or simply trying to defuse the fireworks by putting herself between them and saying, "I love you Daddy," or, "It's okay, Mommy." In other words, Sami acted as Ken and Marie's therapist and "appeaser," trying to force them to regulate their emotions (while not attending to her own) when they didn't do so themselves. In this way, Sami learned to ignore her own feelings, which impaired her ability to appraise where she stands in relation to others—a vital life skill. In short, Sami's self–other balance was disrupted by her internalizing the issues in her parents' relationship—a crazy-making situation that could have become the kickoff for Sami's self-irrelationship.

Fortunately, Ken and Marie came around to realizing what was happening to their daughter and why. Their baseline love and trust for one another enabled them to create a workaround for themselves that took the burden of their relationship off their daughter. This consisted in agreeing to a practice of asking one another for a "time-out" when friction between them would begin to escalate. As they became increasingly skilled at this practice, it had a spillover effect in their daughter's life. From her parents' changed behavior, Sami came to see that, while arguments and other kinds of distress are a normal part of family life, they can be dealt with in ways that don't jeopardize family stability or her own safety.

The experience with the security guard gave Ken opportunity for a time-out—first with his daughter, and then with the security guard.

"Sami, I was wrong when I yelled at that guy. He was only doing what he's supposed to do. It's his job, and I was out of line—way out of line."

"Well, so Daddy, are you going to apologize to him?" Sami asked.

"Yeah. I am," Ken answered. "He deserves it, and so do you."

Ken's coming clean with his daughter and with the security guard will go a long way in helping Sami understand conflict management. But talking about it is only part of the process. She also needs to see changes in behavior and attitude for her to be able to develop a more whole and coherent perspective on human interactions, as well as on conflicts we experience within ourselves.

Kids Aren't Diagnosticians

The above example shows how Sami behaves when home life seems to be threatening to go off the rails. Taking the welfare of her parents and herself into her own hands, she acts to make things better, or at least to divert her mother and father's attention from whatever is upsetting them. Having little frame of reference for how feelings and relationships work, she feels that she *must* do this to make the world safe for herself again.

The implications of living in a world defined by a parent's moods can be grave. If Mom suffers from major depression, the kid lives in a perpetual state of crisis, and even desperation, driving her to take any available measures to ensure that her mom is "okay" so that the child herself feels some relief. The problem is that a child hasn't the experience or skills required for distinguishing between transient and chronic moods, so her reaction to her mother's moods will be the same in either case.

The person invested in irrelationship loses sense of self when unable to act out a do-gooding song-and-dance routine with another person. The person in self-irrelationship has lost the ability to connect even with his own need for contact and connection with others. This split-off state within himself leaves him unable to appropriate his own identity, feelings, needs, or desires—in other words, he's mired in the crazy this book is all about. He's unable to step back and recognize tensions and conflicts within himself and make judgments and decisions that take them into account. He's emotionally brittle and riddled with anxiety, which makes him unable to make sense of his life without resorting to criticism and mistreatment of himself.

A different scenario is possible. Deliberately accepting and making use of internal conflict can give us a flexibility and dynamism that opens the way to creativity, adaptability, comfort with oneself, and connection with others.

Your Feelings Are Going to Come Out Anyway

Our feelings demand expression. When denied they have virtually unlimited power to find ways to show themselves, some quite bizarre. Even dissociation—the most sophisticated of psychological defense techniques—may be enlisted to force our feelings out in the open. As an emotional experience, however, dissociation is less like fear (which it sidelines), and more like an itch we can't get rid of. Though the ostensible purpose of dissociation is to "not be present," the affected person experiences an uncanny sensation that, somehow, things just "aren't right." He may go so far as to create new personalities that become discrete identities, with their own moods, histories, and other identifying features. Psychoanalyst Harry Stack Sullivan (1953) referred to these as "Not-Me" states—states in which we are literally "not ourselves." It's far more comfortable to be in touch with "Good-Me" or even "Bad-Me," but Not-Me is, well, not me. According to Sullivan, the Not-Me is driven by anxiety so powerful it can't be accommodated, leading to a defensive split in oneself that tunes out the craziness.

However, ongoing defense against one's feelings is likely to be costly. Depression, for example, can be used to avoid anxiety, but it can create a sense of deadness in oneself. Or we may refuse to acknowledge anger by turning it inward. The problem with these techniques is that they represent unconscious attempts to force coexistence of Good-Bad, Happy-Sad, or Angry-Accepting, leaving the true experience of ourselves paralyzed, developmentally stunted, and exhausted by the energy outlay necessary just to keep things quiet in ourselves, or, at least, seemingly so.

Some clinicians believe that depression can be used as a defense against awareness of extreme anxiety (Bose 1995, 1998). Depression becomes, then, the one "place" we can go to be cut off from both the experience *and* the expression of feelings. In his essay "Mourning and Melancholia," Freud (1917) suggests that depression is actually an unconscious mourning, and says elsewhere (1914) that the unconscious is the repository of grief experienced early in life, especially that resulting from loss of a loved one. Such loss produces anger at the lost love-object. When the self determines that such anger is unacceptable, the anger is purposely redirected inward ("introjected rage") in order to shut down the self. But shutdown doesn't mean dead. Regardless of how insistently and calculatedly we try to deny our feelings, we can't outthink them indefinitely.

James' story below shows what this can look like.

Feelings Revealed in Actions: Killing Love

James, a forty-two-year-old man, came in for an extended consultation because everything he'd thought about his life and his identity had fallen apart, and yet he found himself falling in love again. Among the reasons this frightened James was that his history told him that, when attracted to a woman, rather than making something romantic happen, he was likely to do whatever it took to kill the relationship.

Working with his therapist, James uncovered a song-and-dance routine he'd first begun to develop at seven years old when his parents' marriage was falling apart. As an adult, this song-and-dance became the device James used to tell would-be girlfriends to "go screw themselves." He dimly perceived that somehow his reaction to the possibility of romance was related to his parents' split-up, which had killed not only life as understood it, but even how he understood himself.

James's parents were both healthcare professionals. His mother, a clinical social worker, told James she'd left his father because it seemed he had very little interest in being a parent to James. Throughout his childhood—and still—she could be overbearing, but she had thoroughly convinced James that any "issues" tormenting him were the result of his father's mistreatment. She quite comprehensively let herself off the hook for James's psychological ill health or well-being. James's father, a physician, suffered a psychotic episode during the divorce. His behavior was so off the wall that it continually humiliated and frightened James, leaving him disconnected from his father and insufficiently concerned about his paranoid behavior. Self-contradictorily, he was resentful that very few people in his family's social circle had any sympathy or compassion for his father but instead shamed him for it.

Despite his mother's opposition and his own confusion, James felt obliged to protect his father from the cruel treatment he was receiving from others, including James's mother. Ultimately, however, his protectiveness didn't prevent his father from ending up institutionalized.

James's personal development was stunted by his having internalized his parents' mutually traumatizing attachment, which itself bore markers of irrelationship. To defend himself, he disconnected from their attempts to make the relationship work while ironically mimicking their repetitive cycle of rupture and repair in his own life. This could be seen in his symptoms: panic attacks that came out of nowhere, episodes of depression, and a pattern of professional success rapidly followed by unintelligible failure. Through it all, he experienced an inability to formulate for himself what was important to him, or even who he was supposed to be.

Still, he continued to harbor the hope that things would somehow work out if he could meet someone who made him feel complete, making his life "okay." And in a way, that's what happened. He again met someone with whom he'd be able to share love, yet almost immediately went to work saying and doing things that would ensure the new romance would quickly devolve into either coldness or acrimony—in other words, would play out as his parents' marriage had years before. Fortunately for James, his latest would-be girlfriend caught on fairly quickly to how James was flipping the cards, and exited within weeks after their first date. As for James, he had finally crossed a line that made him no longer able to deny his own behavior had once again short-circuited his hope for love, leaving him alone with his pain. This time, however, he finally looked for help.

One day at the end of his session, when filling out the check to pay his therapist, James wrote on the memo line, "Bad Therapy." A few days after that session, however, James wrote an email to his therapist that revealed a new willingness to entertain a healthier, more reflective approach to managing his life:

*Do thoughts start emotions or vice versa? What's your line—
"you can't outthink your feelings?" What does that mean? My
behavior will speak, you say. But what is the "no feeling" of
depression? I feel today like I did before I started therapy. It seems
easier to survive if I don't expect to not feel miserable because
then nothing can go wrong, But who wants to walk around like
that? I thought expressing the emotions would dissipate them.
Doesn't seem like it. I need to see progress, but this is more like
charting failure. But being able to write this note tells me that
my own expectations have been limiting my goals. I have, in
fact, been thoroughly committed to failing. What's different is
that I'm now seeing that.*

James had taken a major step toward resuming personal
development that had been interrupted during his childhood, but
had not yet achieved cease-fire between what he wanted to feel
(nothing) and his destructive relationship pattern. The war between
his parents raged inside him, unaffected by his growing, mostly
intellectual understanding of how it had affected him as a child. But,
as the email revealed, he still viewed himself as essentially a failure
and his self-defeating actions as payback for his failures with no
actual reckoning with himself. Nevertheless, his new ability to feel
rage and tell his therapist, his girlfriend, or anyone who cared about
him to screw themselves was a marker of reconnection with himself.
Sooner or later suppressed feelings *will* come out—sometimes in
the form of self-defeating patterns that make us so miserable that we
wall ourselves off in a place of enforced but numbing predictability.
This is craziness, and all of us have a variety of it. What are we going
to do with it?

STAYING ON TARGET

Exercise

Adult Caregiver Responses to Stressful Life Events

The table below gives two examples of stressful life situations that can disrupt relationships. Reading from left to right, note the consequences the individual's response to the situation brought about for her- or himself.

Next, review your own history for similar experiences and recall examples of your response resulting in loss or abandonment of a relationship.

Stressful Event that Made You Feel Out of Control	How Did You Respond?	Outcome
Partner or spouse became unemployed.	I assumed all financial responsibility for the household.	I felt resentful, hurt, and unappreciated. My investment in our relationship diminished.
Money problems.	When I became financially stressed, I didn't allow anyone else know about it.	I left relationships out of embarrassment; I blamed myself for difficult financial situations.

Exercise

Exploring the Influence of Historical Relationship Patterns— Then and Now

The following table gives two examples of negative behavior children witness in caregivers and the negative outcome that experience creates in the child's life as he gets older. After reviewing the two examples, review your own history for points of identification, or cite examples of family relational patterns from your childhood that still affect you negatively.

Relationship Patterns and Behaviors I Saw as a Child	People in My Family Who Were Involved in These Patterns and Behaviors	What Effects Did and/or Do These Patterns and Behaviors Have on Me Now?	What Is My Inner Conflict? How Is This Self-Contradictory?
My parents were constantly fighting, but no matter how ugly it got, they always told me how lucky I was to have two parents.	My parents.	I tolerate nasty behavior in others, especially people I'm involved with romantically, but I never say anything about how it makes me feel. This increases distance and resentment.	
My dad complained constantly to us kids about how difficult living with my mom was, but I never saw them try to work out a problem calmly.	My father.	I stew in resentments toward others. I don't know how to approach an issue calmly to resolve it. If I ever discuss my relationships with others, it's only to complain about them.	

Using the table above, consider the ways that relationship patterns you witnessed as a child play out in how you interact with others now—especially with people with whom you have or have had a romantic connection.

Consider a relevant past or current relational pattern of your own that you can recognize, and answer the following questions:

- What effect is this pattern having on your relationships with others now?

- Where does this pattern come from?

- What other factors exacerbate how this pattern affects your interactions with others?

After identifying patterns in yourself that create distance between yourself and other people, especially those whom you'd like to know better, use the table above to imagine simple behaviors you might use to open a way forward toward connecting with others.

CHAPTER SEVEN

A Good Enough World: Self-Irrelationship to Better Relationships

Blaming the Victim in a "Just" World

The popular but widely unexamined belief that the world is "just" has led to development of the "Just-World Theory," a hypothesis suggesting that dissecting an apparently unfairly victimized individual's behavior will uncover why he's suffering (Lerner and Simmons 1966). Thinking this way allows people who cling to the idea that life is "fair" to deflect their anxiety while creating a wake of blame and guilt for victims of negative events that couldn't possibly be their fault.

One bizarre outcome of this worldview is that some victims of trauma "valorize" their suffering, leading them to construct an identity that includes expecting others to take advantage of them. Such preemptive mistrust undermines our capacity to tell a trustworthy person from a predatory one. This can become internalized as a pattern of self-irrelationship that attracts others invested in similar patterns.

Another undesirable outcome of viewing the world as just is that it promotes the idea that I can make myself invulnerable by always "doing the right thing." This can lead, for example, to the idea that rape victims were "asking for it by dressing that way." A strange corollary of this is that research has shown that women observing a demographically similar group of women working on a problem blamed them for electrical shocks they received for "wrong answers." The observing group even rated the victims as less physically attractive than did a group of women who had not been permitted to observe the experiment (Lerner and Simmons 1966; Carli 1999).

In another study, female and male subjects were told two versions of a story about an interaction between a woman and a man. The versions of the story were identical except for the endings: in one version, the man raped the woman, while in the other he proposed marriage. In both groups, the female and male subjects viewed the woman's identical actions as leading inevitably to the outcome she received, even though the two outcomes were dramatically different (Lerner 1977). Regardless of the cost to others, our anxiety level falls if we believe the world operates fairly, and that we can control outcomes in our lives. The downside, of course, is that if something bad happens to me, it's my fault. This can be carried so far that an individual may come to believe that he can't survive if the world *doesn't* operate this way.

My perspective of how the world operates is intimately connected with the relationship I had with my primary caregiver, whom I depended upon to keep my world "safe." But what becomes of the badness I experienced as a child—the negative characteristics and behavior of the parent I did everything I could to placate? It goes to the only other place available for a child: onto myself. And if taking this "badness" onto myself becomes accepted as necessary for my survival, "bad" becomes a core aspect of how I view myself as an adult. For example, if my mother was abusive to me, I deserved it, and I *must* hold on to that idea if the world is going to make sense to me, and, more gravely, if I'm to survive.

The internal dialogue of song-and-dance recreates such childhood family drama, leading to self-blame, and even a twisted pride at one's own victimhood, that is self-reinforcing and attracts others into irrelationship-based connection with me.

A Contract to Fix My Bad Behavior

A kid living in a household with an abusive and rageful caregiver can conceive of only one explanation for the caregiver's violence: he has done something wrong, which proves that he's bad. An abusive parent isn't a dependable guide for leading a child toward a healthy perception of himself often because of the parent's own history of trauma. This is one way that trauma can be passed across generations, leading to the installation of "bad-me" identities of self-irrelationship in the child. Since he's vulnerable and has no other frame of reference, the kid has no choice but to internalize the reality he's living in, meaning he has to manage his parent's loss of control by managing his own behavior in whatever way he can. This is the only alternative the child has for constructing a world that makes sense to him.

As this kid gets older, he'll manage his relationships with everyone around him in much the same way in order to keep his world predictable and safe. Coercion and appeasement will act as "stand-ins" for justice, while compassion and integration are kept in the wings for fear that his own unconscious feelings will upset the balance of his world. Denial and dissociation ensure that his "deals with the devil" stay below the radar, passed off by others as part of his personality, and by himself simply as part of how the world is. In self-irrelationship, we unconsciously confine ourselves to relationships with people who go along with these negative, self-protective expectations.

How we make sense of the world depends on the belief that we can know the mental state and intentions of others, and that even unintended consequences of a person's actions make sense in a just world. So we assume that people do what they do because of "who they are," without considering that other factors may be involved. For example, a friend may not pay his share of a restaurant tab, leading me to label him a cheapskate without my allowing for the possibility that he's financially distressed but too embarrassed to let anyone know it. My resentment continues to build as this scenario is repeated over several social get-togethers, until finally I explode, forcing the friend to reveal his financial predicament. Though the truth is finally out, the damage—possibly long-lasting—has been done to our friendship. This bias, known as the "fundamental attribution error" Ross (1977), the "correspondence bias," or the "over-attribution effect," leads us to insist on a just universe early in life and to continue the habit unconsciously.

The flip side of justice-inducing song-and-dance routines is that, when the caregiver accepts the child's routine at face value, he is deliberately using the kid to make himself feel better by avoiding curiousity regarding the more profound implications. Like the child, the caregiver makes an attribution error that causes him to view the child's behavior as a function of "who he is," rather than considering the possibility of a warped developmental reality forced on the child. For both, the routine becomes a way of life grounded in an unspoken bargain neither is aware of, based on assumptions having to do with justice and victimhood. The kid will continue negotiating similar relationships throughout his life in order to feel secure.

Pattern Recognition: "Where Have You Been All My Life?"

The short answer is, right here—right here in my own head, history, and life, including every relationship, and beginning with how I adapted to life with my mother. I've found people who will fit into my song-and-dance and not paid any attention to those who won't. Crucially, what we are attracted to about the other in the beginning is what kills the connection in the end. By not sharing myself meaningfully with others, I devalue them, causing them to resent me. When they call me out on it, the connection collapses.

During his 2008 presidential campaign, Barack Obama often used the slogan, "We are the ones we've been waiting for!" However, this can also describe my dark, repetitive patterns with significant others. When I find a familiar *you,* I have also re-found the familiar *me*—the parts of myself that I've split off from my consciousness in order to survive. In the realm of self-irrelationship, this corresponds with what Freud called the repetition compulsion. It can be compared to the definition of insanity popular in twelve-step programs: repeating the same thing over and over, expecting different results. In a repetition compulsion, a person repeats a traumatic event or its circumstances over and over.[1] This includes either reenacting the event, or putting oneself in situations where the event is likely to occur again. This "reliving" can also take the form of dreams in which memories and feelings of what happened are repeated.

Learning to differentiate oneself from others in healthy ways is a key developmental accomplishment which can be impaired for those who have internalized traumatic experiences due to ineffective parental care. The rift between parent and child becomes a part of one's own identity, in the form of internal conflicts and divisions.

Song-and-dance routines are a powerful means of dissociating the related anxiety, but are hard to identify and overcome so I can create new ways of relating that feel safe in an unpredictable world. Ironically, allowing myself to experience and reveal my fear and vulnerability seems to be the only way to overcome this anxiety.

How We Find Each Other

Relationships grounded in irrelationship are founded on unspoken contracts we make with each other—sometimes before we actually meet. These contracts stipulate that "I'll be exactly who you need me to be so you can play out your internal drama, on condition that you'll do the same for me." Superficially, self-irrelationship attracts others to us who meet our expectations, healthy or otherwise. The attraction may seem like magic, bad luck, or even karma, but it's based on specific factors such as how we see ourselves and others, how we view reality, and how we make decisions to determine the course of our lives.

This idea broke in on a woman who had been in therapy for several years because of her repetitive cycle of failed romance. Finally, one day it clicked for her: "I have a man living in my head!" This was the beginning of her becoming able to see that not only had she internalized her parents' dysfunctional relationship, but her experience growing up had crucially colored how she saw other couples. She cynically believed that apparently happy couples must be faking, which only supported her cynicism. This finally brought her to realize that she had "a woman living in her head" who was looking for the man living in her head. Once this idea dawned, she began to open to possibilities other than those entrenched in her unexamined assumptions about the world.

By whatever means, we *do* seem to find the same thing over and over. As conventional wisdom puts it, birds of a feather flock together. However, a conundrum arises when we consider another piece of conventional wisdom: "Opposites attract." How do we resolve this apparent contradiction?

People affected by self-irrelationship look for others who are both similar to and different from themselves. The particulars of how one's self-irrelationship meshes with another person's reflects how sharing the experience of trauma draws them together into a song-and-dance routine. This doesn't mean that some aspects of their attraction can't be healthy, but playing up the healthy aspects so they become part the new and improved way of operating will be complicated by their traumatic history until they jointly work out its irrelationship overlay, and why each was looking for it to begin with.

The Red Ball

Desire pulls us toward one another. However, this is often experienced more as drive than simply desire. Cultural theorist Slavoj Žižek presents an example of the difference between desire and drive in his book *The Parallax View* (2006). He describes a little girl trying to grab a red ball. Capturing the ball is her goal, but her hands are small and the ball is big. Every time she reaches for it, the ball slips away. She chases it around the room, but the same thing keeps happening. Still, she wants the ball so that she can feel mastery and competence. Besides, it's pretty, and she wants it.

At some point, after having her desire repeatedly denied her, she realizes that trying to catch the ball is fun, which suddenly transforms her desire. She starts giggling while she chases the ball, and without realizing it becomes more interested in chasing than possessing the ball. In other words, her drive is about *not* reaching her goal. A sadomasochistic relationship with desire isn't a necessary outcome of such a scenario, but it's pretty common among people invested in irrelationship, revealing both its unconscious motivation as well as anxiety resulting from traumatic conditioning.

Now, let's put this in self-irrelationship terms. I see you across a crowded room. I don't know what it is, but I sense something about you that's partly desire, but also a "special something" that is *not* okay, but that *I can fix.* So I'm driven toward you. However, at the same time, I also sense an unbridgeable gap between us that convinces me that I *can't* have you.

Obviously, this isn't about "you" and "me," but about my using my need for closeness to play with and then deny the idea of actually being with someone who truly seems desirable. In reality, however, I not only hold back from approaching that person, but I don't even allow myself to experience *within myself* the idea of desire. I may harbor within myself the idea that another person could make me "whole," but even that is walled off and remains unexplored. No sane relationship of any type can take place until I allow myself to acknowledge the conflicted and conflicting parts of myself—a.k.a. my crazy. Starting to call those things by their right name is the beginning of letting anything else in.

The Line Must Be Drawn Here!

Kevin was hungover and still a little drunk from the night before.

"The line must be drawn here! No more!" he said.

He had just come from court, where his second divorce was being arbitrated after a three-year marriage.

Kevin, a man in his early forties from a middle-class family, had worked at the Belgian consulate in New York for a decade. He didn't know that "The line must be drawn here!" is well-known among *Star Trek* fans as coming from Jonathan Frakes's 1996 movie *Star Trek: First Contact*. Captain Jean-Luc Picard is referring to the invasion of the Enterprise by the Borg—perhaps the ultimate alien-villains of the *Star Trek* corpus.

In the movie, Captain Picard is captured by the Borg and assimilated, becoming Locutus, the mouthpiece of the Borg, who communicate to humanity that our time is up! Having had his humanity taken away, Picard is forced to do terrible things, all the while knowing he's doing them. And, as the Borg tell him, he finds that, at least initially, "Resistance is futile." Well, our song-and-dance routines can be compared to an assimilating Borg invasion against which resistance has been futile for a long time.

Picard rarely loses his cool, but when threatened by the possibility of repeating the Locutus role forever, he explodes, "The line must be drawn here!" just as Kevin did after his court appearance.

"You killed me!" Kevin mumbled to his therapist as he clutched his head in anguish.

"What?" his therapist responded.

Kevin had been in therapy off and on for several years, but had never mentioned a traumatic incident from twenty years earlier, the memory of which was triggered by his traumatizing deadlock with his wife. Kevin moved to New York from Belgium with his best friend when they were in their early twenties. His friend was severely depressed through his teenage years, and Kevin had taken it upon himself to be "the only one" who was there for his buddy. Their move to New York was partly an "antidepressant treatment" Kevin had suggested so that his friend could get away from his severely abusive family. A few years into their new life in New York, however, Kevin's friend disappeared, leaving a note that read hauntingly, "You killed me!"

Did he commit suicide? Kevin had wondered.

The answer turned out to be yes. His friend had jumped off a bridge in another state, and his body wasn't found for three months. During those three months, Kevin fantasized that his friend had escaped out west, "maybe to Arizona." When he found out what had happened, the ambiguity of the note his friend left for him made him wonder what part he played in his friend's death.

When Kevin was a school-aged child, his mother was diagnosed with bipolar disorder so unstable that she often required hospitalization. The young Kevin often sneaked out of the house where he lived with his father and younger brother to visit his mother in the hospital. Sometimes they played a game where Kevin would pretend to kidnap his mother. In fact, once he actually did "kidnap" her: he sneaked her out and off the hospital grounds, which led his mother to tell him, "You've saved me!" However, the game didn't play out as he'd hoped; the hospital caught his mother and brought her back, worsening her anxiety and mania. Kevin's father punished him.

As time went on and the frequency of his mother's hospitalizations increased, Kevin became increasingly interested in—in fact, driven by—wanting to see how far he could get his mother from the hospital before they were stopped, and how much could he "help" her during those periods of "rescue." In short, he was driven by the "game" rather than by the outcome.

In the end, none of this worked. His mother was ultimately institutionalized, leaving Kevin believing that the only thing that would "save" him was true love. Long before he met his second wife, he had developed a preoccupation with finding women who, he said, "needed his help."

When Kevin began therapy, he was severely depressed, drinking heavily through his first divorce, and had so little energy that some days he couldn't get out of bed. His depression not only ruined his marriage but threatened his job, which was a condition of maintaining his immigration status. He was unable to see it at the time, but the reason his first marriage ended was because his wife had somehow "gotten well." When they met, she was one of Kevin's typical "love" objects: anorexic, depressed, and addicted to cocaine. She was a model, which Kevin believed put her well out of his league, but perseverance paid off and they were married.

They lived a party lifestyle, with Kevin increasingly captivated by the feeling that his wife was dancing on the edge of a cliff. Enraptured as he was, Kevin felt that if he could not save her, they'd go off the cliff together. Instead they went into couples therapy. His wife went to rehab, kicked her addiction, and made real progress on her eating disorder. As if on cue, Kevin suddenly lost interest in their marriage.

Kevin's depression continued, becoming so severe at one point that he was hospitalized. Then he met Avery, the woman who became his second wife. Avery had also just gone through a divorce and was a great comfort to him. After about a month, he felt he could confide in her about some indiscretions that had occurred near the end of his first marriage.

Suddenly Avery became obsessed with Kevin in ways that reminded him of how his mother used to howl for him from the hospital, as if her well-being depended on his care for her. The information about his history that Kevin confided in Avery primed her deep-seated fear of unfaithfulness. She began calling Kevin's therapist, begging him to assure her that Kevin wouldn't be unfaithful to her, so that she wouldn't be so anxious.

Just as Kevin had played a kidnapping game to save his mother, had moved to another country to save his best friend, and had agreed to live a careless lifestyle to save his first wife, he devoted himself to reassuring Avery that his love was the remedy for her fear and insecurity.

When Kevin's therapist suggested that Kevin was once again repeating his song-and-dance routine, he insulted his therapist for doubting the reality of his love for Avery, and stormed out determined to prove that his resistance was not futile, and that his care for Avery would not be assimilated by the Borg inhabiting his marriage.

About three years later, Kevin called his therapist to ask if he could come back into treatment. Predictably, Kevin's pitch to make true love real to Avery hadn't worked. She continued to suspect Kevin of infidelity, and physically attacked him and even one of his female coworkers. Then one day his own increasingly violent feelings triggered his remembering the story of the little red ball. Shortly after that, he came home from work to find that Avery had knowingly and sadistically left him, leaving a note that repeated what his friend had said years earlier:

YOU KILLED ME!

Upon reading this, Kevin said, "The line must be drawn here!" and called his therapist the next day.

Kevin never caught the ball, but continued chasing it from one doomed relationship to another, all of them including some combination of the themes of murder, suicide, or insanity. In the end, however, Avery's improbably worded note jarred Kevin into wondering if he could just let the little red ball roll on without him.

In-Out/ Up-Down/ Near-Far

Many of us chase the little red ball in different kinds of routines as we move, now closer, now further away from actual intimacy. Shelly Goldklank (2009) conceptualized a dynamic relationship system as part of her approach to treating couples. These relationship dynamics are at play in each of our most intimate relationships:

- In-Out: Are you, and is your partner, actually in or out of the relationship?

- Up-Down: Who's exercising the most power?

- Near-Far: How much intimacy are you able and willing to tolerate?

The dynamics and the patterns from our relationship history become part of how we interact in every relationship. Since patterns of interaction seldom remain long in one place, they're unlikely to settle into a stable, predictable pattern. Even if we resolve the initial dynamic tension around whether we are actually in or out, we can emotionally exit the relationship or refuse to challenge ourselves, each other, or the relationship so as to sustain ongoing emotional connection. We may avoid issues of power and intimacy without resolving them. In short, we can be out without knowing it. And, in fact, out is the only dynamic position in a relationship where the connection can settle into apparent stasis. From there, the only place to go may be the next relationship, where all of this gets played out yet again.

A relationship that has a true life of its own never settles into a *state* of being. Instead, it's constantly being formed, reformed, challenged, stimulated, and pulled back from psychological defense systems that include running away, freaking out, and running back. And this brings us back to the process of *rupture and repair*. Rather than landing in a perfect attunement in and connection to others, we can, in this way, co-create the ongoing development of "good enough" ways of caring for—and being cared for by—each other. This is far more useful to our psychological health than an impossible search for perfection.

Anatomy of Irrelationship as Self-Protection

A significant aspect of the self-irrelationship system is the apparent mistaking of *sympathy* for *empathy*. Empathy is the ability to feel what another person feels and appreciate what it's like to be in her life. Sympathy, sometimes called *cognitive empathy*, gives consideration to another's experience without feeling it. Empathy requires investment, rather than the safety of distance that sometimes even includes patronizing sympathy. Empathy also connects us ethically with the other person's suffering, laying the groundwork for compassionate action. Cognitive empathy, on the other hand, can be used to manipulate others as much as it can be used to relate.

Now—what is intimacy?

Intimacy is connection between two people that allows sharing of vulnerability. It includes our experience and perception of what and who we are—what we think, what we feel, what we've done. It risks the sharing of the admirable, the reprehensible, or the humiliating, regardless of the cost.

Intimacy is *not* simply telling another person your darkest secrets. It's the unfolding and sharing of life that comes about as two people learn over time who each other really is. Put more bluntly, intimacy isn't my telling you that I can span the whole spectrum that runs from insensitive to casually cruel at times, but (unintentionally) *letting you see it for* yourself as we live our lives together.

To explore self-irrelationship, I have to ask what it means to be intimate with myself and try to figure out why I avoid it. Avoiding intimacy with myself involves dissociation from my true feelings about pretty much everything—positive, negative, or traumatic— ending in my having no perception of anything about myself, especially my own vulnerability.

Intimacy means being open with those parts of myself—not all at once, perhaps, but building a trusting dialogue of self-disclosure within myself. It involves emotional risk and, sometimes, grieving for or coming to terms with the unhappy or unattractive parts of myself as I reappropriate them. Ultimately, accepting all of myself unconditionally is a joy that nothing outside me can shake.

STAYING ON TARGET

My Agreements with the World

Development of a song-and-dance routine involves making agreements with our environment. The primary agreement is to care for my caregiver so that she can make it possible for me to survive on my own. In later life, this becomes the cornerstone of self-sufficiency. Over time, I continue making similar agreements, so that wherever I go, I ensure the world is safe for me. However, this involves splitting off essential parts of my "true self," particularly those related to my genuine needs and desires. The table below gives examples of such agreements:

Agreement	How It Plays out in Relationships	Impact on Myself
I will make myself the solution to the problems in my partner's life.	I feel resentful for being burdened with your problems; you feel resentful at my devaluing you and seeing you as "needy."	I (or we) don't look for real solutions to problems. Instead, my caretaking deflects focus from 1) our real conflicts, and 2) my real needs as a person.
I contort or deny my feelings to ensure that my caretaker feels what he does for me meets my needs.	I feel unheard and don't know why I'm in this relationship, but feel I can't leave.	I feel devalued and subtly resist caretaking the way others devalue or resist what I have to offer. I avoid thinking about what I'm feeling.

Using the above examples, think about agreements with others in your own life and how they play out.

- What benefits do you get from carefully structured connections with others?

- What aspects of these agreements leave you with negative or uncertain feelings? Describe those.

- Discuss ways that you "make do" with caretaking others offer you, especially how this results in your *not* having your needs met.

CHAPTER EIGHT

Self-Irrelationship
Success and Failure

The "Other-Woman" Anniversary

"Hey, Doc," said Kylie, "It's our anniversary!"

"Oh yeah? You and who?" her therapist asked.

"Who you think? Certainly not Elizabeth! We've been together too long to celebrate anniversaries. It's Sherry—it's *our* two-year anniversary!"

Kylie and her partner Elizabeth have an "open relationship," with one not-easy-to-keep rule: no falling in love with anybody else. Kylie's attitude reveals a seeming lack of remorse for her ongoing violation of that rule.

Kylie's relationship with Elizabeth looks a lot like a caretaking routine: two people orbiting each other in a committed domestic partnership while seeking sex elsewhere—an emotional defense with unapparent roots.

Kylie's father died suddenly when she was five, leaving her with a hole in her life, her mother bitter and depressed, and both with the task of raising her younger brother. Kylie made a point of bending over backward to help her mother feel better, mostly by not demanding anything from her. Left on her own, she bonded with other would-be parent figures—teachers, coaches, other kids' parents—figures who, in some manner, made her feel cared for and loved. Kylie's mother unconsciously signed on to this alternative parenting agreement with the proviso that Kylie would never give her mother reason to believe she wasn't a good parent. This protected Kylie's narcissistic mother from awareness of her own fragility, and forced Kylie to maintain the appearance that "everything's fine."

"Does anything about celebrating with Sherry seem familiar to you?" asked her therapist.

"What? You mean celebrating with the 'other-woman' instead of with Elizabeth? Why is that a big deal all of a sudden?"

"Maybe telling yourself it's 'not a big deal' *is* the big deal," her therapist challenged.

"Like how?" Kylie asked, almost belligerently.

"Like by not getting caught breaking the only rule of your 'open relationship.' It's sort of like not letting your mother know how you depended on other adults when you were a kid. I wonder if, down deep, you were hoping your mother would find out and get mad. And I wonder if part of you would like Elizabeth to find out about Sherry and blow up at you. Seems to me that you're letting both of them get away with not seeming to care about you."

Kylie couldn't think of anything to say.

"I'm sure that, despite your living arrangement with Elizabeth, you feel neglected a lot of the time—even when Elizabeth's in the apartment with you. But you haven't ever said so to her. To me, that sounds a lot like the deal you made with your mom after your father died.

"But there's something else," her therapist went on. "When you did that deal with your mom, it was a way of sidestepping grief—one of many examples of how you've walked away from your feelings over the years. So when I asked you just now if all this seemed familiar, you almost went off on me, but then dialed it down to a 'so what?' like it doesn't really matter."

In a self-irrelationship routine, I'm performing for myself (as well as others) to convince myself I'm okay—that I have everything I need. At the beginning of her session that day, Kylie was excited about her date with her "other woman." But when her therapist compared it to how she'd long related to her mother, she stifled an impulse to go off on him while minimizing the split-second flareup of anger. Her therapist didn't let her off so easily.

"What happened to your excitement about seeing Sherry tonight after I brought up your mother?"

"Well, okay, at first I was mad at you," she admitted. "But then—it didn't take long, really—I felt this sadness, I guess, because I've been with Elizabeth for so long, but we don't seem to feel we have anything to celebrate. And, well, also, Sunday was the anniversary of my dad's death, and I still don't like thinking about that."

"Yeah, your father broke a rule. Parents aren't supposed to leave their kids when they're little. What's a kid supposed to do with that? It just leaves them afraid of getting close to *anybody*."

"Yeah, it was bad. At school too because my friends stayed away from me—the kid whose dad died. I couldn't really blame them. How are they supposed to know what to say? And poor Mom was a wreck. I couldn't tell her about it. I didn't have anybody to even talk to but my teachers and, later on, one or two of my friends' moms."

In self-irrelationship, we recreate and enact traumatic scenarios over and over again without even knowing we're hurting, which just keeps old wounds fresh with no opportunity for them to heal.

"I'm really glad we did this today, Kylie. You've opened up something that you haven't been able to look at. If we stay with it, it can make a huge difference in your life. What is this like for you right now?"

"Well, when I came in I was so excited, or anyway, I thought I was. It's weird how pulling in what happened after dad died knocked the wind out of me. You had me feeling like crying like I never was able. Ever."

"Well," her therapist answered, "maybe you'd like to start thinking about who you want to tell about your dad—Elizabeth or Sherry. I've got no advice to give you about that right this minute, but it's a *big* one—one of the biggest you'll ever have. Good luck," he smiled.

The Irrelationship Trust Fund

"I don't trust him."

"I don't believe anything she tells me."

"She lies all the time."

"You can't believe anything they say."

"They'll make promises, but that's as far as it'll ever go."

What does it mean to trust someone? How does Kylie tweak the idea of trust in her relationships with Elizabeth and with Sherry? Whatever idea of trust is being lived out in those connections is influenced by the history of each person involved, and then turns into something that doesn't have much to do with what most of us think of as trust, i.e., the confidence that another person won't lie to, cheat, or mistreat us.

My trust for others may be based on first impressions, or it may develop gradually from living with or around them. If I've experienced trauma, "trust" may not capture how difficult it can be to permit myself to get close to others. Traumatic experiences may leave me feeling unlovable, afraid of betrayal, and expecting others to reject me or worse. Yet opening up to others who reciprocate and with whom I'm compatible is necessary for intimacy to develop. It also includes accepting the inevitability of future loss which may repeat the pain of loss suffered in the past, or may even be worse.

In a twisted way, song-and-dance routines of self-irrelationship can be "trusted" the same way an abused person "trusts" his abuser, and excuses her by telling himself she can't help it. The person enacting irrelationship keeps faith by behaving exactly as expected, for good or for ill. Similarly, self-irrelationship serves long-standing needs for safety from painful feelings by walling them off so they aren't recognized. This deprives me of being able to recognize who I am and what I need to be a healthy, functioning person.

Acting Out the Song and Dance

As noted earlier, a song-and-dance routine is a means of acting out anxiety so that we aren't aware of it. Unfortunately, this also makes it hard to feel joy or other feelings, because the brain doesn't easily select which feelings to tune out. But what do we mean by "acting out"? Acting out is behavior that obliquely displays my real feelings without my realizing I'm doing it. Early in life, I hide uncomfortable feelings so my caregiver will remain comfortable and able to care for me. If my caregiver is abusive or neglectful, I'll probably become numb to all my feelings, except when badly regulated emotions take over and are displayed in exaggerated waves of despair or joy. This mechanism is sometimes driven by drug or alcohol use, excessive sex, or other mechanisms that betray internal fragmentation. Or it may be as minor as nonverbal behaviors, or saying one thing when my facial expression or other behavior says something different. Sometimes I may identify so closely with my "acting-out" behaviors that I accept labels that describe the behavior—labels such as "Do-Gooder," "Fixer," "Martyr," or other GRAFTS behaviors that in self-irrelationship I perform internally for my hypercritical mind's eye. In self-irrelationship, these behaviors are intended to fix *myself.* Over time such "self-parenting" routines become disguised as good self-care—routines such as a healthy diet, exercise, abstinence from alcohol, or carefully managed dating. However, this won't reverse the internal self-defeating patterns that leave me feeling guilty, ashamed, and emotionally hungover. Nevertheless, I ultimately will "mature" into someone who has structured my whole life around dysfunctional behaviors I adopted in childhood so my world wouldn't fall apart.

The Family Drunk: What Happens When I "Succeed" in Fixing Someone Else?

Ray was reflecting on the confusion he experienced when his mother stopped drinking. "I didn't know it at the time, but when my mom got sober, it ruined my life. Her drinking was the one thing that let me feel safe."

Irrelationship easily lends itself to combining with other compulsive addictive behavior, such as heavy drinking, drug use, compulsive sex, binge eating, and others. These combinations are hard to work through, and feature major characteristics of addiction and obsessive-compulsion, including entrenched, repetitive thoughts and behaviors, unrest, empty or lonely feelings, pain, and helplessness.

While relationship issues don't meet current psychiatric diagnostic criteria, they're analogous to behaviors seen in self-irrelationship, including its destructive impact on an individual's life. Severity of self-irrelationship can be classified as mild, moderate, or severe, according to criteria used for substance use disorder.

Features of Substance Use Disorder

Criteria (APA 2013) for diagnosing a substance use disorder are:

1. Taking the substance for longer periods and in larger amounts than intended.

2. Desire to curtail or reduce substance use but inability to do so.

3. Obtaining, using, and recovering from substance use occupies increasing portion of the individual's time.

4. Continual or recurrent cravings and urges to use.

5. Use of the substance disrupts performance of ordinary activities and obligations associated with normal routine in the home, school, and workplace.

6. Persistent use despite problems in relationships related to using.

7. Gradual disappearance of social, occupational, or recreational activities in favor of using.

8. Repeated use of substances despite dangerous situations that may develop around using.

9. Continuing to use despite psychological and physical problems related to using.

10. Need for increasing amounts of substance to obtain the desired effect ("increased tolerance").

11. Development of withdrawal symptoms, which are relieved by taking more of the substance.

Ray continued: "Just before my mom got sober, there was practically nothing left of our lives. We were the center of each other's universe, but that was about it. Then, all of a sudden, other people started coming around—her sponsor, other members of AA—and all they talked about was being sober. Some said that helping my mother helped *them* stay sober. It was obviously a good thing for her life, but it pretty well ruined mine."

Ray's relationship with his mother seemed to all but disappear when she started going to Alcoholics Anonymous. But it created a second layer of crisis for him in the sense that the developmental framework within which he had operated practically all his life had vanished without warning. Relationships similar to Ray's with his mother underlie self-irrelationship: the relationship with the primary caregiver is distorted because love and nurture aren't available for the child, which makes the child's environment unstable and frightening. Ray's mother needed treatment for alcoholism;

however, her drinking wasn't something that "just happened," but was driven by her own developmental trauma. For both, unresolved trauma played out in substance abuse. Getting sober began the process of his mother's becoming stable enough to work out her other issues instead of avoiding them. It also posed new challenges in terms of learning to recognize and allow new possibilities for herself as well as for Ray. Prior to that, though, discontinuity in the external world became internalized, with serious impact on sense of self, relations with others, and other aspects of living in the world. This is where substance use disorder and self-irrelationship overlap, resulting in a form of PTSD referred to as "complex PTSD," or CPTSD.

Complex PTSD symptoms include social and interpersonal avoidance, feeling cut off from others, never feeling close to another person, and negative self-concept including worthlessness and guilt. While survivors of PTSD may feel "not myself," survivors of complex PTSD may feel no sense of self at all, or experience a changed personality.

Unresolved Trauma and Irrelationship Routines Sustain One Another

Compulsive behaviors and the physiological effects of alcohol, substances, gambling, and food binges don't just underlie, but reinforce song-and-dance routines to maintain the delusion that we're sharing our lives with others.

"It was just us against the world," Ray continued. "And though I complained about it a lot, well, that was our world, our home. My mom was the house drunk, but she was *my* house drunk. The school even called Protective Services on her and were talking about taking me away from her, which scared me, both because I couldn't live without her, and I *had* to believe that she couldn't live without me. I knew it was on me to keep her safe, and the way she drank, that kept me pretty damn busy."

"You-and-me-against-the-world" became Ray and his mother's irrelationship routine. His mother's drinking made healthy development impossible for Ray, so he adopted a GRAFTS routine to keep his mother "safe" while dulling his own feelings. Perhaps even more to the point, he needed her to keep drinking so that he had a reason to keep his attention focused away from how she was damaging his own life. So her going to AA felt like a betrayal, much like what happens when one member of a couple figures out she wants something more out of life than their scripted song-and-dance routine. Doors open, and emotional unpredictability is exposed. Unresolved issues, pain, fear of loss, and sadness surface, seemingly out of nowhere. This destabilizes their shared commitment to irrelationship. Break-up isn't inevitable, but, one way or another, change is coming.

"When my mom quit drinking, she knew I wasn't a hundred percent happy about it. Sometimes she'd sneak off to meetings and lie about it. Meanwhile, I started drinking because I liked the head it gave me, like out to lunch—way out to lunch. Oh yeah, part of me knew I was drinking because I resented how my mom had 'left me,' and that she was getting better without my 'help.' Then somebody suggested that I try Al-Anon, and I went, even though I was still drinking. That was how I began to see how Mom started abandoning me when her drinking took off when I was a little kid. Well, it turns out her getting sober aggravated that resentment. Anyway, somebody in Al-Anon finally got me to try AA. When I told them I'd been going to Al-Anon, they started calling me a 'double-winner' because I was getting sober, dealing with my mom's drinking, and finally dealing with her and me getting out of our crazy caretaking routine. So, well, the way I look at it, that makes me a triple-winner!"

Ray's story illustrates how drinking and drugs feed compulsive caretaking routines, which in turn drive drinking and drugging. In tandem, they had stunted Ray's development, leaving him with deep-seated interpersonal issues that, without intervention, would probably have followed him for the rest of his life.

The Cost of Success

Belief that song-and-dance routines "work" is an easy-to-expose delusion. Consider the idea of power over someone else's feelings. Can I really create a lasting emotional state in someone else by the way I behave toward him? Most of us know that emotions don't work that way. Emotions reflect what's happening in the world inside and around us. Healthy people don't get frozen in any kind of permanent emotional state. Imagine a person who has the same emotional response to anything that happens to her, for example, joy at loss of job, of a girlfriend, upon hearing of a loved one's death, or seeing her child go through the pains of growing up. The idea is absurd, except in the case of the person suffering from true chronic depression. However, for the sake of the discussion, suppose that I do "succeed" at making Daddy "happy" every time I perform my song-and-dance routine, inspiring me to take my show on the road for the rest of my life. How would this shape my personality, perception of myself, and how I relate to everyone around me? This is the backstory of self-irrelationship: self-punishment replaces self-compassion.

As an infant, everything I knew about the world was learned from being in my caregiver's arms. In that setting I learned that if I giggled, it made mom's face change from a scary one to one that comforted me. As I got older, I kept giggling to make others feel better, regardless of what was actually happening around us. And I *still* use that giggle to make myself feel better, and even give myself a feeling of power. As I grow older, I may figure out that the whole thing was fake, but I still remember that it worked when I felt uncomfortable so I continued using it. What's harder to get my head around is that I still compulsively use that feel-better giggle to make myself feel better.

The Cost of Failure

Suppose my giggling routine didn't work: I used it on Mom, but she didn't seem to feel any better afterward. She just kept looking the way people look when they're having a hard time. This disappointment dogs my life, so that even as an adult, when others seem uncomfortable it makes me feel uneasy. So I set out to fix whatever is going wrong in their lives. And I'm so good at finding people to do this "to" that I forget about my own unease and my unhappy memories. Or, if uncomfortable feelings do break through, I chalk it up to personal failure.

So the outcome of my self-irrelationship is one of two grandiose delusions. Either I teach myself to believe that I *did* fix my caregiver, and can go out into the world fixing anybody, or I believe that everything going wrong around me is somehow my fault. The common denominator of the two delusions is the belief that it's my responsibility to fix everything going wrong around me. I even take that idea into how I view and manage my own life: I compulsively pursue the idea of "perfect," be it perfect mind, body, spirit, or life—whatever idea of "perfect" I'm invested in. And I do this without any insight into how pursuing perfectionism walls me off from who I really am—in other words, is a symptom of self-irrelationship.

Intergenerational Transmission of Failed Song-and-Dance Routines

"It wasn't until my father was well into his seventies," Thomas reflected, "that we were able to have anything like a real relationship.

"I'd been in therapy for years trying to make sense out of my ongoing self-sabotage. I did it again and again through my twenties and thirties. It didn't make sense and everybody knew it, including me. Until then, I believed someone had the answers: my father, his father—more recently, a therapist. I got an MBA from a prestigious school and plenty of great opportunities, even after word was getting around that I was something of a screwup. And it kept happening—I just couldn't get myself together.

"My therapist and I had gone over different aspects of my history again and again. Finally, my father and I had some long talks after his heart attack when he was seventy-five. That was when I started noticing that some parts of his story sounded an awful lot like mine. And his family history even more so. Looking back now, it seems strange how long it hadn't clicked for me how similar our stories were."

Compulsive caretaking routines can manifest powerfully in unlooked-for places. As a matter of course, we expect psychological defenses to kick in when we're having serious problems in important relationships. But it often doesn't register when defenses pop up destructively in our everyday lives. Somehow the day-to-day emotional discomforts, or even disasters, that are part of "normal life" don't stand out for us as signals related to long-standing unresolved issues. Researchers have demonstrated that our patterns of relating to, understanding, and interpreting one another are passed along from generation to generation (Sette et al. 2015), and there is growing evidence that anxiety, to a significant extent, is also learned by children from parents (Eley et al. 2015).

"Time and time again, my therapist and I went over what I thought was the biggest issue of my life: how controlling and demanding my father was. It took a long time for me to realize that the way he acted wasn't just some inborn personality trait. Something had happened to him to cause it. As it turned out, it was a leftover from his own upbringing—his history of being a compulsive caretaker for his own father. It took some time, but realizing that about him brought me up against a pretty unattractive truth about myself: the more I tried to escape from my father, the more I became him."

Thomas's father grew up on a farm in the Midwest in the 1940s. He'd always wanted to join the air force to become a pilot, but his mother and father had other ideas. Though poor, they saved and sacrificed so that at least one of their three sons could be the first in the family to go to college. As religious people, their heart's desire was for him to come back and teach at the parochial school, and eventually become the school's principal—a job with immense prestige in their community.

Sadly, but with obvious relief, Thomas summed it up: "The failed banker who wanted to be a doctor repeated the story of the failed teacher who wanted to be a pilot, who repeated his father's failure. Finally—my father and I can relate to each other!"

Thomas had a good chance of breaking the chain and passing along a more connected way of caregiving in his relationships by making a decision for genuine intimacy with his father.

Intergenerational (or transgenerational) patterns of trauma will be transmitted fully, absent successful intervention. Patterns of relationship carry on in either-or ways. The son doesn't want to be like the father, and the father, rather than being too harsh, is too lenient. Or he is harsh—but "never hits his kids"—giving him a sense that he is different while at the same time remaining abusive in other, more socially acceptable ways.

Traumatic transmission also shapes relationship patterns and patterns of identity, suggesting that self-irrelationship is inherited: the apple doesn't fall far from the tree. If one generation passes the buck, the next generation may do the cleanup work, or not.

The Good, the Bad, and the Ugly

From what we've seen in this chapter, irrelationship-driven caretaking, successful or not, isn't going to make me happier or better adjusted. In fact, successful caretaking is harder to treat, because if I'm convinced that my song-and-dance routine works, I have no incentive for shifting attention from "What's wrong with you that I can fix?" to "What's happening with me that needs to be fixed?"

This book provides a framework for refocusing away from my delusions and onto accepting the walled-off parts of who I really am that make me uncomfortable. Calling those things by their right names is the first step toward living with myself insightfully and empathetically. It's how I find my way out of depression, isolation, and loneliness.

The following chart illustrates the hopelessness of both "successful" and "unsuccessful" caretaking outcomes.

The Good	The Bad	The Ugly
My anxiety is relieved.	Something doesn't feel quite right.	I'm by myself and depressed.
My routine is "working."	Something still doesn't feel quite right.	No one *really* appreciates me.

How will we know when the jig is up?

Knowing when the jig is up is challenging because my self-protective relationship with myself is, itself, the jig. Though it's hard to spot, certain markers will inevitably appear. Recognizing them for what they are brings home a certain threat that my life is in danger of being upended, which, naturally, is anxiety-provoking. Calling them by their right name, then, can be almost heroic, and deciding to change will probably feel scary. But it *can* be done.

Windows of Opportunity

When my behavior causes those around me to think I'm someone "special" who should get "special treatment," I'm at risk for turning their "accommodating" me into an isolating straitjacket for myself, because it allows me to continue living on the periphery of my own life without looking at what's really happening inside me. Occasionally, though, I may catch a glimpse of a different idea of how I might "be" with others, as well as a breakthrough of the feelings I've kept at arm's length that point to how I've allowed old resentments to keep me from meaningful connection with myself and others. Making even a tentative decision to stop brushing away those feelings could be the moment I start letting myself into my own life.

STAYING ON TARGET

Willingness to Let Go

Parting with my obsessive-compulsive routines will feel at first as if I'm dropping all the protections anyone needs to get through life. However, the aim isn't exposure to harm, but learning a different way of managing life as it really is.

This exercise will help you assess how willing you are to begin stepping away from self-defeating protective routines and engaging the world. The following table provides spaces for listing self-irrelationship-based behaviors and, next to them, possible alternative behaviors that could replace dysfunctional ones. Following the examples given, list behaviors of your own, or even thoughts you have, that may be self-confining; then next to them list possible alternatives.

Self-Irrelationship routine I can see in myself	Behaviors and ideas that could replace this routine
Examples: • I beat up on myself when I make mistakes—sometimes for years afterwards. • I'm determined to come off as the "good guy" when working out conflict with someone else, but for some reason, I feel bad about myself afterwards.	*Examples:* • Accepting that I'm not perfect: I make mistakes like everyone else, but my life can continue on anyway—like everyone else's. • Recognition that conflict arising from different ideas and needs is a normal part of everyone's life, and nobody has to be "right" or "wrong."
1.	1.
2.	2.
3.	3.
4.	4.
5.	5.

PART III

BENDING, BLENDING, AND MENDING

CHAPTER NINE

Self-Self Assessment: The 40-20-40

Given what we've learned so far about how self-irrelationship cuts us off from ourselves, leaving us feeling "crazy" in all the wrong ways, it's time to take a look about how to further the process of self-reflection and repair. Bending, becoming more emotionally and psychologically adaptive, flexible, and open-minded; blending, developing ways to recognize and include all aspects of who we are and could be in our self-identity, rather than being driving mad by experiences of fragmentation; and mending, allowing past wounds to heal, engaging in the work of repair and recovery, both personally and in relationships with others. In order to do that, we have been building self-compassion. Now, it is time to look more deeply at how we can gently interrogate the schisms within which divide us against ourselves.

The 40-20-40 establishes a safe space for us to interact with others and to be present with ourselves so that we can undercut our song-and-dance routines.[1] In fact, presence with oneself makes presence with others possible.

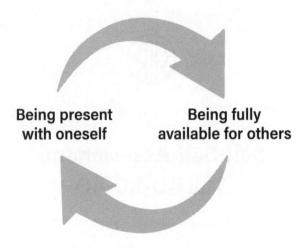

**Being present
with oneself**

**Being fully
available for others**

Rather than making interaction with others a zero-sum game of winners and losers, the 40-20-40 makes winning possible for everyone. Instead of depleting resources, availability to others replenishes them while also accommodating healthy solitude when wanted or needed. For couples and larger groups—friends, family, work teams—the 40-20-40 provides a safe framework for understanding interpersonal difficulties without resorting to shame and blame.

Asking myself "What's my part?" in conflicts, problems, or issues is a pivot to creative resolution. The 40-20-40 helps users to do this by allotting 40 percent of resources and responsibility to each party, while reserving the 20 percent "in the middle" as a "space" for listening and negotiation. The 40 percent is based on two-party conflicts, but any size group can adapt the practice to ensure that all members are able to safely articulate their needs and feelings, with the middle 20 percent reserved for working out a meaningful, respectful resolution, or at least taking steps in that direction.

In the practice, each individual is given an equal, timer-managed opportunity to speak, maintaining focus only on her or his own experience in the conflict. When not speaking, other members practice listening with openness and hospitality, with an eye to how others' experience affects them and how their own thoughts and actions may contribute to the conflict. Finding fault or looking to assign blame are out of place. The purpose of the exercise is to ensure safety and build trust, so that mutually constructed solutions can be developed that take each participant's feelings into account. In 40-20-40 parlance, this is known as "expanding the middle," or building "us-ness" in a relationship—that is, caring for the *relationship itself* as a discrete entity which the couple or group values and nurtures.

A usually unlooked-for outcome of practicing the 40-20-40 is that dissociated parts of ourselves gradually emerge from the shadows, or even burst onto the scene, to our surprise and even delight. Overwhelming anxiety is ratcheted down to manageable levels so that we can accept parts of ourselves that we'd locked away.

Acceptance of oneself and others goes hand in hand. An important piece of this is dropping the habit of being nicer to others than I am to myself, and coming to view myself as "just another person." This compassionate detachment may unexpectedly help me see myself for who I really am, freeing me to be more loving and more available to others.

The 40-20-40 Model of Relationship

The 40-20-40 was developed to help people repair the split between self and other as revealed in actually occurring relationships. Janina Fisher (2017) states that "in order to unconditionally accept ourselves . . . we need to develop a relationship with *all* of us: to our wounded and needy parts, to the parts hostile to vulnerability, to the parts that survived by distancing and denial—to the parts we love, the parts we hate, and even the parts that intimidate us" (78). This book recalibrates the 40-20-40 to repair the self–other split *within the individual* in order to undercut compulsive caretaking routines performed *on oneself.*

How does the 40-20-40 do this? Our earlier books show how the 40-20-40 explores "my part" in dysfunctional relationships with others, as well as how I view and engage (or don't) the world generally. This book applies the 40-20-40 to myself *as an individual* to see how I've cut myself off from my own feelings, making me unaware of important parts of myself and my functioning so that I may even be clueless that anything is wrong. This leaves me prone to view everything that happens to me in one of two ways: 1) Somebody else ruins everything, or 2) I ruin everything. Predictably, this is liable to make me crazy.

The 40-20-40 uncovers how I act out the Performer/Audience paradigm within myself. The Performer-me (40 percent) has taken charge by imposing a malign construct on the world that keeps the Audience-me (another 40 percent) from "knowing" parts of myself I've cut off (dissociated) from my consciousness. The 40-20-40 enables me to identify the "what" and "why" that the Performer and Audience are committed to keeping in the dark, which has the effect of keeping me walled off from others. The "middle 20 percent" is the blame-and-punishment-free zone I can choose to enter (probably haltingly at first) to work all this out. As I get used to doing it, the process itself makes the doing less frightening, and puts me on an increasingly secure footing for engaging both "the real me" and "the real world."

What does this look like in practice?

Imagine a line that separates *you* from *the world*, that is, from anyone or anything around you that suggests the possibility of actually involving yourself in some type of relationship. It could be with an individual, a group, an organization—anyone or anything that might interest you. For the sake of this discussion, let's say that a new coworker with whom you've shared a polite greeting and chatted briefly has signaled openness to knowing you better. You're sitting opposite that person at a ten-foot-wide table bisected by a line that leaves five feet of space in front of each of you.

You	Midpoint	The Other
0 Feet	5 Feet	10 Feet
0 percent	50 percent	100 percent

Next, imagine expanding the width of the line in the middle of the table so that it occupies an area 20 percent of the width of the table, leaving 40 percent on each side of the midline.

You	Expanded Middle			Me
0 Feet	4 Feet		6 Feet	10 Feet
	40 percent	20 percent	40 percent	

This graphic illustrates a dynamic that two people may share, but may be more broadly seen as illustrating the interaction between each of us and the world we live in—the ways in which, in my own mind, I'm constantly keeping score by assigning responsibility, blame, and criticism for whatever goes on around me. However, the rules of the 40-20-40 sideline the idea of blame. That doesn't mean that the 40-20-40 takes away my feeling anxious or vulnerable, but it does create a space for me to look at those or any feelings I have, and how that affects my interactions with the world. The goal isn't for me to beat up on myself, but to trace how upsetting experiences early in life taught me to see the world as bad and everyone in it as at least potential adversaries. I learned to walk through life defensively while pushing my *real* feelings and needs into the background ("split off"), so that I don't feel unsafe and wary of others.

The magic of doing the 40-20-40 with myself is that it helps me:

- Discover ways to manage anxiety that I couldn't conceive of when I first started using my internal song-and-dance routine.

- Repair the split within myself and with others by making a gentle, non-critical, even curious reappraisal of how I view myself and others so that I can see how conscious and unconscious choices I've made *within myself* have kept me isolated and crazy.

- Take a new look at how the style of interaction in my family of origin caused me to ignore my need for nurture and care.

- Come to see and accept myself and what I "come from" as they *really are*—probably the most vital single step toward a new, freer life.

- Use these newly developing perspectives to create open-ended alternatives to the self-irrelationship pattern and my stultifying view of myself.

Implementing the 40-20-40

The 40-20-40 can be used both for quiet self-exploration during downtime at home and as a "rapid-intervention" tool when you're in any kind of situation that makes you feel uncomfortable. Escalating emotions can be tamped down by identifying what's going on "in you." This by itself is often enough to restore rational thinking and choice-making. Habitual practice will create new habits of "self-talk" as well as change how you view and describe uncomfortable situations, which promotes generosity and accountability toward yourself and others.

The following describes the structure and ground rules for using the 40-20-40 as a spot-check inventory when I need to hit the pause button, figure out my part in a provocative situation, and respond thoughtfully instead of reactively.

- Imagine hitting a pause button and saying to yourself, "This is getting scary/disturbing/infuriating. *What do I need right at this moment* to get through it comfortably?"

- Try to identify the feelings that are coming up for you: "This is pissing me off," or "She's making me uneasy," or "He shouldn't talk like that." When you can, sit in a quiet place and write down what was going on and how you felt at the time. This will help you recognize similar situations and feelings in the future.

- Feelings don't have to be justified or excused. They are simply part of what happens in you and are entitled to respect. If looking at them via the 40-20-40 isn't feasible right at that moment, make a plan to do so when you're able. If judgmental language toward yourself comes up, note that and include it in your 40-20-40.

- With practice, examination of negative experiences will empower rather than trouble you, and self-understanding will replace rumination and self-punishment.

- Repair using the 40-20-40 will spill over positively into other parts of your life, so welcome opportunities to use it, even though it's sometimes a painful nuisance.

- The 40-20-40 is a *practice*, so getting the knack of it will take time. But it yields positive, durable changes in you that improve your overall functioning.

- Internal communication—Me-meeting-Me—replaces self-irrelationship—the craziness that grew out of our isolation, demonstrating van der Kolk's (2014) description of "communicating fully (as) the opposite of being traumatized."

- Doing the 40-20-40 will sound crazy at first. Let it. This is how you learn to know and love the person you are.

STAYING ON TARGET

Exercise

Practicing the 40-20-40 with Myself

Imagine and anthropomorphize the split-off, dissociated parts of yourself—parts of you that represent denied needs or desires, aspects of your life that you're uneasy about or dissatisfied with, even things about yourself that you just don't like. Visualize these as other "yous" sitting in chairs at a ten-foot-wide table with a line drawn down the midpoint, leaving five feet between each of you and the middle.

You (Caretaking)	Midpoint	Split-off You (Isolated)
0 Feet	5 Feet	10 Feet
0 percent	50 percent	100 percent

Next, imagine expanding the width of the line in the middle of the table so that it occupies an area that's 20 percent of the width of the table, leaving 40 percent on each side of the midline for each imagined "part" of yourself.

You (Caretaking)		Expanded Middle		You (Isolated)
0 Feet	4 Feet		6 Feet	10 Feet
	40 percent	20 percent	40 percent	

Now imagine sitting at the table "with" the split-off parts of yourself and interacting with them in the way you might do with someone you know but haven't seen for a long time, or even are just meeting for the first time. How would the conversations(s) begin? What would you want to know? What reactions do you imagine yourself having as you come to re-know parts of you that you've avoided or been afraid of?

Exercise

Asset Mapping

This exercise looks at how our personal attributes affect our relationships with ourselves and others. In each section below:

- List the positive and negative personal attributes you believe have an impact on how you function in the world.

- Reflect on the "negative" items you've listed to uncover how they cause problems for yourself or just make you feel uncomfortable.

- Reflect on how you could use your "positive" attributes to help you accept, reinterpret, and even change parts of yourself you're unhappy with.

Capacities, Gifts, and Skills

1. What attributes in yourself indicate self-acceptance and sanity? How do they affect how you see yourself and interact with others?

2. When and how do you stop yourself from applying these positive traits when it comes to your conception of and attitude toward yourself? How does how you view yourself relate to your experience of isolation, loneliness, and craziness?

3. How could you use the positive attributes you've named to reduce your negative attitude toward yourself? How could doing this make you feel less isolated?

Commitment

1. What concrete actions could you use to begin taking accountability for your part in the isolation you experience in your life?

2. What kinds of things do you do to avoid accountability for your part in relationship issues or conflicts?

3. How could you use actions you listed in Question 1 to counter your avoidance of taking accountability for your part in issues with others?

Authenticity

1. When you notice that you're diverting your attention from discomfort you feel, what actions can you take to allow yourself to experience what's actually happening inside you? How could acceptance of discomfort and vulnerability improve how you feel about yourself?

2. What behaviors (for example, denying or minimizing problems you have with others, or trying to placate them) do you use to avoid looking at how you're feeling or behaving? How does this disconnect you from others?

3. How could acceptance of your uncomfortable feelings, your vulnerability, and your "imperfections" help you to connect with others?

Meeting Needs

1. What kinds of things do you do for yourself to meet your needs?

2. What behaviors do you use to distract your attention from your needs? Or to prevent others from knowing about your needs and helping you to meet them?

3. How could you use items identified in Question 1 to undercut denial of your needs as suggested in Question 2?

Decision-Making

1. When you have an important decision to make, what do you do to reduce your anxiety so that you can feel better about your decision?

2. What behaviors do you use to avoid difficult decisions and choices? Are you aware that you're doing it when it's happening?

3. What anxiety-reduction practices could you use to make it easier to make difficult decisions?

Emotional Openness

1. In what circumstances and situations are you willing to let uncomfortable feelings come to the surface? In what situations do you feel you can safely share your feelings with others?

2. What circumstances and situations make you unwilling to let uncomfortable feelings come to the surface, or to tell others about them?

3. How could you use the insight about your comfort with sharing feelings to improve your willingness to share feelings in uncomfortable situations?

Following Through

1. What things do you need—feelings, resources, support—in order to follow through on decisions and commitments?

2. What kinds of things make it hard for you to make decisions and follow through on them?

3. How could you use items you named in Question 1 to help you move past the issues or obstacles you named in Question 2?

Sharing

1. What is it like for you to give to others? To receive from others? What makes these experiences meaningful and satisfying?

2. What interferes with your ability to share with others, or a specific other who comes to mind? What relationship experiences do you recall as having been unsatisfying, or leaving you with negative feelings?

3. Think of a person with whom you are in the process of building trust. Imagine using information that came up in Question 1 to change an unsatisfactory outcome from Question 2. How might reflecting on giving and receiving impact a simple conversation, or a more significant encounter, with that person?

Fellowship

1. Many of us experience feelings of both interest and unease when we encounter new people. What feelings come up for you in such situations?

2. When encountering new people makes you uneasy, what do you do to keep them—or yourself—at a distance?

3. How could you use both the positive and negative feelings identified in Questions 1 and 2 to reduce anxiety and create trust between yourself and others?

Conflict Resolution

1. When you've been involved in conflicts with others, how did you and the other person(s) involved manage the conflict so that it had a satisfactory outcome?

2. When you've encountered conflict you didn't want to deal with, what words or behaviors did you use to avoid dealing with what was happening? How did you feel afterward?

3. If you find yourself in a conflict with a person with whom you're building trust, what behaviors identified in Question 1 could be used to resolve the conflict and increase the trust between you and that person?

Crisis Management

1. When you encountered a serious crisis in a significant relationship, what did you do to get through the crisis? How did it leave you feeling?

2. What behaviors do you perform (alone or with others) that prevent constructive crisis resolution?

3. Imagine a crisis arising between you and a person with whom you're beginning to build trust. How could information identified in Question 1 be used to disempower dysfunctional behaviors identified in Question 2 so that, after the crisis has passed, the two of you aren't left with unresolved issues?

Stress Regulation

1. When you feel stressed, how do you prevent those feelings from escalating into conflict with others?

2. Which behaviors do you use to avoid dealing with stress?

3. How could you work together with someone with whom you are building trust to use items that you listed in Question 1 to improve on items in Question 2?

Intimacy

1. What words and behaviors do you use to communicate to others that you accept them as they are?

2. What behaviors or mechanisms do you use to avoid risking rejection by others?

3. When working on a project with another person, how can you convey to them your commitment to that person and the project, while remaining authentic about your feelings of anxiety and vulnerability?

Boundaries

1. Which words and behaviors do you use to indicate respect for healthy boundaries—yours and others'?

2. What incidents in your history suffered from boundaries issues that got in the way of sharing and intimacy? What did that look like?

3. In working with someone with whom you're building a trustful connection, how could you use items identified in Question 1 to lessen the likelihood that items identified in Question 2 will get in the way of your connection?

Acceptance

1. Give examples of times you were able to safely discuss a negative experience of, or with, another person.

2. Give examples of times that you shied away from discussing a negative experience with another person because you were afraid of how they would react.

3. Imagine how you could safely bring what you learned from experiences listed in Item 1 to make it less likely that you (and the other person) will be left with unresolved negative feelings.

Nurturing a middle ground in which I can genuinely experience myself clears a space in which the world as it is can be encountered and negotiated. Probably the most important learning point in this practice is becoming able to do it without finger-pointing, which doesn't solve anything for anyone. Dismantling self-irrelationship involves putting aside the compulsive caretaking that stands in the way of a true encounter with myself—the only possible grounding for living authentically in the world.

CHAPTER TEN

Making Your Crazy Work for You:
The DREAM Sequence

DREAM is an acronym for the five steps for recovering from the "crazy" of self-irrelationship. These steps—Discovery, Repair, Empowerment, Alternatives, and Mutuality—enable users to reconnect safely with parts of themselves they had pushed out of their awareness as a result of early life trauma.

According to van der Kolk (2014, 205), "The challenge of recovery [from trauma] is to reestablish ownership of your body and mind—of your *self*. This means feeling free to know what you know and to feel what you feel without becoming overwhelmed, enraged, ashamed, or collapsed." The DREAM Sequence is a recipe for recovery from the brainlock of commitment to the *not-me* delusion of self-irrelationship, enabling me to accept myself as I am and deliberately make use of my vulnerability as a recovery tool.

While each step of the process builds on the one before it, the steps overlap with and reveal more about one another. For example, Discovery is the initial phase of learning about how the way I live *in myself* prevents my experience of my own feelings and needs. Articulating this *to myself* undercuts the anxiety created by my unmet needs, which allows me to go forward with Repair in order to meet those needs. The DREAM Sequence, then, is a phase-based approach based on well-defined models[1] that promote recovery from complex trauma.

Discovery can also be viewed as a game-changing tipping point resulting from the experience of hitting rock bottom. Once I begin to discover what's been happening inside me, denial becomes increasingly difficult to return to and sustain. As I begin the Repair process, Alternatives—new choices—will appear that will make my life as I've been living it increasingly unattractive. Transformative change is usually an evolutionary process that unfolds in unpredictable growth spurts and plateaus, which overall proves to be well worth staying in it for the long haul.

The Five Phases of the DREAM Sequence

Discovery
Recognizing what's been happening

Repair
Beginning to heal

Empowerment
Feeling hopeful that we can do the work

Alternatives
Identifying and using better relationship tools

Mutuality
Consolidation of feelings of togetherness into sustainable mutuality

The DREAM Sequence	
Step 1 **DISCOVERY**	• Recognizing I've been enacting an irrelationship song-and-dance routine within myself to keep from recognizing my own feelings and needs; seeing how that keeps me disconnected from others.
	• Discovering irrelationship mechanisms that keep me disconnected.
	• Noticing when feelings of anxiety and isolation break through and overwhelm the surface calm of irrelationship
	• Realizing the song-and-dance routine isn't working anymore, opening me to the possibility of change.
	• Coming to see myself as having different facets and layers, some of them related to dissociated trauma.
Step 2 **REPAIR**	• Using the 40-20-40 to uncover how a song-and-dance routine traps me in fake self-sufficiency and cuts me off from my real feelings and needs.
	• Allowing myself to experience repressed feelings and open up to repairing the split within myself.
	• Viewing disturbed feelings in myself when encountering others as a marker of lost parts of "me," and as an opportunity for repairing the split by reconnecting with those feelings.
	• Viewing disturbing encounters with others as opportunity for repair through honesty about my feelings, especially vulnerability; seeing how this helps overcome the crazy in me that keeps me separate from others.
	• Gaining insight into how hiding from connection with myself and others distorts how I see myself and what I can offer others.
	• Practicing viewing "crazy" or "broken" parts of me as opportunities for change and growth.
	• Valuing my feelings and using them to gain insight into how I treat myself and others.
	• Sidelining the idea of "blame," and approaching my interior life with curiosity and unconditional compassion.

The DREAM Sequence	
Step 3 **EMPOWERMENT**	• Accepting that what I have always done isn't what I always have to do. • Developing insight into how my song-and-dance routine stands in the way of knowing myself. • Seeing accountability for my choices as liberating rather than punishment. • Using what I learn in the 40-20-40 to build positive self-talk and self-care routines.
Step 4 **ALTERNATIVES**	• Seeing change as part of the excitement of being alive, both in myself and in the company of others. • Reappropriating and re-viewing split-off parts of myself as opportunities for self-knowledge and growth. • Reframing personal dependency and interdependency as being deeply human, and as reasons for gratitude that displace delusions of self-sufficiency. • Growing the practice of resorting automatically to the 40-20-40 to deal in real time with anxiety, anger, and conflict. • Moving beyond the need to use positive self-talk, to automatically knowing how to manage both joy and challenge. • Experiencing negative insights into myself and personal feedback from others as opportunities for change and growth.

The DREAM Sequence	
Step 5 **MUTUALITY**	• Re-encountering and partnering with split-off parts of myself with a whole feeling of union with myself that's unconditionally and limitlessly hospitable to others. • Embracing vital, unpredictable, and even unhappy parts of life as they come. • Becoming increasingly excited by relationships in which feelings, power, and vulnerability are shared freely. • Enjoying a free flow of giving and receiving in my relationships that includes giving and receiving of help when needed, without fearing compromise or deprivation. • Making the 40-20-40 part of daily living, sharing, and accountability. • Continuing growth in relationship sanity with myself as practiced in these steps, including seeing it as a precious gift to be shared generously with others.

Patient Zero Redux: Irrelationship, Self-Irrelationship, and How the DREAM Sequence Cracked It Open

Our earlier books recount how Glen (Irrelationship Patient Zero) got himself into two marriages that were crucially affected by irrelationship, but with two dramatically different outcomes. Now we'll explore how Glen's self-irrelationship protected him from his split-off feelings while he and his second wife, Mai, were working though the song-and-dance routine that was haunting their marriage.

The self-irrelationship split acts as a stop-loss for the effects of trauma caused by ineffective parenting. It does this by dissociation, which leaves a developmental deficit to be addressed later in life—or so one hopes—but meanwhile, for better or worse, becomes part of the bedrock of character development. (*Character* may be understood here as including the totality of one's psychological defense system.) The means or motivation for escaping this defended position is sometimes compared to the addict's image of "hitting bottom," i.e., finding yourself left with no choice but to let go of denial, face your issues, and explore alternatives to "doing what you've always done." The threshold for making this choice ("surrendering") varies from person to person, depending on personality factors such as open-mindedness, anxiety level, and the individual's level of self-hatred and impulse toward self-destruction. Some individuals, in fact, do not survive hitting bottom, opting instead for death by slow or rapid means. Choosing whether or not to die is, then, the most significant, and perhaps most frightening, moment in the battle.

Discovery

Discovery is the most important step in the DREAM Sequence. It's the tipping point at which I begin to restore long rejected and forgotten parts of myself to my awareness. Tenuous at first, the process of recovering split-off experiences may sometimes tempt me to turn and run, but each time I restart it becomes less daunting. That's when my crazy begins to work for me.

How did Glen come to realize that the trauma of his early childhood had caused him to hide parts of himself *from himself?* And how did he come to understand that hiding from himself was self-destructive?

Speaking with his therapist from his bottom of numbed emotional depletion, Glen posed the question, "Is preventing anybody else from helping me or even doing anything nice for me the same as wanting to hurt myself?"

"How would that be?" his therapist asked.

"Well, I know it's messed up, but let me tell you what actually worked, or almost—in a messed-up way. I remember the first time that I got drunk when I was a teenager. I felt this unexpected release—like, *I'm free.* I got sick, threw up, the whole nine yards. But even though it was embarrassing, I also remember thinking that, finally, somebody would have to take care of me! But this is what's *really* messed up: That first drunk happened on a hunting trip with my father! In fact, *he* was the one who got me the beer and booze! It seems kinda sick now, but for years after, I thought that getting me drunk was how my father showed me he loved me!" Glen paused. "Anyway, at the time, nobody else—including my mom and dad— offered me anything better. So what did I have? I hated school, so I played the tough-guy and ignored my teachers, and there weren't any other adults in my life except that once or twice I had sex with the mother of one of my girlfriends. She told me I was a real stud, and I told myself the same thing. That was about as close as I came in those years to having an adult in my life.

"One time, long before all that craziness was in full swing—I think I was eleven—I was filling the bathtub one night when I got the idea that if I could just put my face under the water long enough, I could make myself not feel anything anymore, because I wouldn't exist anymore."

At eleven years old, Glen was looking for a way to get rid of his crazy, even if it meant dying. And this ongoing search for a way out of his crazy culminated in his marrying his first wife, Vicky. She complemented his need for escape by not making emotional demands on others, including Glen. By that time, Glen had made not making emotional demands on others his overriding life strategy: his life before his marriage was a long line of near-miss relationships, wrecked initially by his keeping a distance from, and finally by driving away, anyone who tried to get close to him. This treatment left most of its targets baffled and wondering if he'd ever really cared about them. However, it perfectly suited Vicky. Their marriage blew apart rapidly when, as he neared his bottom, Glen tried to confide in Vicky his almost desperate feelings of emptiness and vulnerability.

Her response was to flee their marriage, which fortunately prompted Glen to flee into therapy.

The DREAM Sequence proved to be the bridge between Glen's bottoming out on irrelationship involving Vicky, and building relationship sanity with Mai. Beginning with discovering how he'd been trapped in his own dissociative process since childhood, the Sequence enabled Glen to piece together how irrelationship dynamics operated both in his own head and between himself and others, especially would-be intimate partners.

Repair (Interactive)

Repairing the self-self split is the jumping-off point of making my crazy work for me. It starts with developing the habit of compassionate self-recognition. Learning to be present with myself paradoxically breaks me out of isolation by enabling me to choose other, non-self options, including leaving the GRAFTS behaviors behind.

Hitting bottom made Glen willing to explore how he played out song-and-dance routines in his own mind and all kinds of day-to-day situations, from over-tipping taxi drivers to indulging family members who, at holiday gatherings, endlessly repeated old resentments against other family members. Undoing these routines requires practice of the 40-20-40 with himself, with the twist that, when making a criticism of others, even in his own head, he asks himself, "What's *my* part in what's going on here?" This proactive method stops the process of putting down others by clearing up the confusion *in me* through interactive repair *with myself.*

Careful examination of one's thoughts and choices may at first seem strange and require deliberation and conscious commitment. But practice will make it part of your habitual interface with the world, so that issues and problems are increasingly easily recognized as they approach, and treated constructively and compassionately, instead of from an adversarial posture that requires a winner and a loser. This changes the world into a dramatically more hospitable place to live.

Empowerment

Empowerment is the product of 40-20-40 self-interactive repair, and is exciting and heady. Finding out that I don't have to feel and live the way I always have changes how I feel about my own humanity and my place in the world.

The 40-20-40 showed Glen the destructiveness of cutting himself off from others and priding himself on his phony self-sufficiency. This was brought home most powerfully by the realization that his marriage to Vicky included a tacit agreement not to reveal vulnerability or to require support from one another—in fact, the opposite of empowerment.

Empowerment is both personal and interpersonal. It gives me resilience, optimism, and openness to possibility, while increasing both flexibility and the ability to maintain boundaries so that others' issues don't disturb my equanimity or equilibrium. Interpersonally, empowerment sharpens my ability to see others' crazy for what it is, but with compassion, without my feeling I have to "fix" it for them. I can be present and supportive without feeling drained, becoming anxious, or placing blame.

As he dissected his marriage to Vicky and his relations with pretty much everyone else, Glen developed the capacity for "reflection-in-action," which is just a fancy way of saying he got better and better at recognizing his old ways from the old days and making better choices for getting through today's difficult situations. Recognizing my crazy, and using it as a guide for choosing clarity and openness instead, is the essence of empowerment.

Alternatives

Alternatives are the fruit of empowerment—the realizing of new choices that empowerment enables me to envision and articulate for myself. As the word suggests, this includes flexibility, trial and error, regrouping, and choosing again if warranted or desired. Living in the idea of alternatives includes willingly living with uncertainty, ambiguity, and waiting. Tolerating ambiguity allows me to choose to make use of uncertainty. As Keats puts it:

> "I mean Negative Capability, that is when man is capable of being in uncertainties, mysteries, doubts, without any irritable reaching after fact and reason."

Increase in self-awareness increases acceptance of others. This allows for reencountering and reintegrating traumatic experiences, including those that led to post-traumatic stress disorder. The 40-20-40 may indeed trigger emotions related to trauma, but growing self-acceptance guides and buffers the re-relating process so that the self-against-other can be reconfigured as part of the new wholeness of self-with-self.

What did this mean for Glen? It meant he was less driven to use caretaking behaviors to divert others' attention from himself. "It was a scary time," Glen told his therapist, describing a conversation with an old friend from school. "Doug knew both Vicky and me, was surprised when we split, and of course he wanted to know what had happened. Well, probably for the first time in all the years I've known him, I let Doug in on what had been happening inside *me* instead of just being someone on whom he could unload his problems. I can't tell you how weird it was at first, having Doug listen to *me* when I tried to explain what the hell happened to my marriage. But the kicker was what he said as we were leaving the café; he said it was the closest he'd ever felt to me! It had nothing to do with who was to blame or giving advice or anything like that. He was just *there.* And it finally—finally—came to me in a flash. Not only can I let Doug get close to me, but when things are going bad for me, I don't have to tough it out by myself!"

Mutuality

Mutuality is the avenue of true engagement and intimacy. In mutuality, I forget about the parts of me and my past that drive my song-and-dance routine. It involves giving and taking, and it grows out of genuine regard rather than the need or desire to use another person.

Self-irrelationship doesn't erase mutuality. It prevents me from even considering it, because of how scary it is to let anybody else see how vulnerable I am, much less depend on them to help me get through tough times.

"Well, Doug turned out to be a better friend than I knew to ask for, or to let him or anybody be in the past. He just listened while I tried to figure out the mess left in my head when my marriage broke up. And it's a good thing I was ready to try, because I brought that mess with me when I met Mai. Well, amazingly, Doug stayed with me, hung with me, and loved me through all of it. I could *never* have allowed anybody to do that in the past—friend or girlfriend. And oh boy, is it a good thing I did, because when Mai and I started getting serious—which was immediately, actually—some pretty hairy stuff started coming up almost out the gate.

"At first, I didn't feel right about dumping on Doug every time we met. But he always made a point of letting me know he valued the way I trusted him. I'd never been able to let another person be with me that way. I'd always had to do all the 'being with,' and had never had a clue how important *accepting* care is to loving someone."

STAYING ON TARGET

Exercise
Old Wounds

This exercise is a practicum for moving beyond old wounds to realizing you don't have to feel what you've always felt, or do what you've always done.

Think back on encounters you've had with others that seemed both exciting and frightening—encounters that may have had the potential for friendship, love, perhaps even just the pleasure of sharing a cup of coffee.

Similarly, recall an experience of interaction with another person that, after it had ended, left you feeling alone or abandoned, perhaps because feelings of unease, fear, or vulnerability led you to disguise your interest in the other person with a song-and-dance routine.

How do you react to such experiences? Can you remember any of the following?

- Increased heart rate.

- Changes in your breathing.

- Tension or pain in your body.

- Sudden recollections of painful experiences from the past.

Now, revisiting the scenario of missed opportunity, imagine yourself consciously accepting your need for human contact and disclosing it to another person. Imagine that this other person receives your disclosure of vulnerability with kindness.

How does reimagining the incident in this way change the experience in your body and mind—heartbeat, breathing, physical discomfort, and painful memories?

What do you think would happen if others in your life—family, neighbors, coworkers—were truthful with themselves and others about this most human need of having oneself accepted?

Using paper and pen, take some time—perhaps twenty to thirty minutes—to write down whatever comes to mind about what the journey through this book has been like for you up to this point.

CHAPTER ELEVEN

Discovery of the Self

One of the key insights to be gained during the Discovery step of the DREAM Sequence is the lack of compassionate empathy for oneself. This is revealed both in how I deprive myself of kindness in day-to-day life, as well as in denial of my basic human needs. Such failure of self-recognition leaves incoherent the sense of self necessary for the healthy development of personality, which includes rationality as well as healthy emotional stability and regulation. Instead we grow our own crazy through dissociation, denial, and projection.

Another part of our humanity that's easily lost to irrelationship is playfulness—a trait seen in all mammals as well as humans. For children, play is a part of learning. As adults, playfulness keeps relationships fresh, joyful, and open to exploration. Without it, they wither.

In professional relationships, play is generative, enlivens creativity, and promotes teamwork. On the other hand, if trust is breached, play is liable to degenerate into bullying, malicious teasing, and harassment, often hidden behind the excuse that "I was just kidding." In individuals, humor toward oneself can be revelatory and playful, or it may be grim, self-deprecating, and hostile, to the point of standing in the way of intimacy.

Reconnecting self-with-self by connecting with my anxiety and vulnerability can be terrifying, or it can be mediated by compassionate empathy. The story below about Kathy and her mother shows how gratifying it can be to take on others' burdens and without ever letting them forget how "generous" I am. Such "playing the martyr" can be a great place to hide from myself and others.

Reciprocity and Its Discontents

Kathy's mother is a saint. Just ask anybody in her neighborhood, at her kids' schools, in the organizations she volunteers for—anybody. Anybody, that is, except her family—especially her daughter Kathy.

Generous as Kathy's mother seems, her resistance to letting anybody do anything *for her* is a wedge between herself and her family. And yet, oddly, she flips from self-sacrifice to hostility if her family doesn't make enough of an outward show of appreciation of her incessant doing for others. When this happens, she feels guilty and out of control afterward; but rather than telling anyone else about these feelings, she retreats further into her isolating song-and-dance routine. In other words, she's a classic Performer.

Looking back on her growing-up years, Kathy couldn't remember ever being told about the importance of reciprocity in human relationships, intimate or otherwise. Nor could she remember being told that her own desires and feelings were important. Instead, her mother warned her repeatedly against getting into relationships with others that could put her "under obligation" to them. A consequence of this was that Kathy learned that with relationships, appearances are more important than what's actually going on in them.

The study of relationships shows that reciprocity creates a bond of trust and respect between involved parties. This is as true in international relations as it is in intimate relations or within families. A vital aspect of this is that opening up—self-disclosure—builds intimacy, as research has demonstrated (Waring and Chelune 1983).

Why do we often find it difficult to maintain satisfaction in relationships, even with people to whom we feel emotionally committed? Why is reciprocity so easily lost or poorly understood, and what is the connection between reciprocity and relationship satisfaction?

The reading and the exercises in this book will impact my capacity to relate to others, to receive from them, and to appreciate and value them. And that's the catch for Kathy's mother. Not allowing others to give to her removes the risks connected to valuing, and therefore being vulnerable to them—a lesson she learned as a small child in her family of origin.

Psychoanalyst Harold Searles (1975) says that human beings are born with the need and desire to take care of others. Even small children, reacting to what they perceive as unhappy facial expressions or behaviors in their parents, will adopt behaviors they hope will make the caregiver feel better. In fact, research has shown that infants of nondepressed mothers are able to tell happy from neutral facial expressions, whereas infants of depressed mothers cannot do so (Bornstein et al. 2011).

Attachment theory tells us that development is bidirectional—that parent and child evolve together, setting the stage for what happens in the child's relationships as an adult. Children raised in families with poor boundaries or permissive or authoritarian parenting are more likely to get into emotionally abusive adult relationships (Beyarslan and Uzer 2020). On the other hand, healthy interdependence with the primary caregiver sets us up for relationships that feature the ability to give and receive care, and share intimacy throughout our lives.

"It's scary—that's what it is!" Kathy said, reflecting on reciprocity. "Giving and taking means I'm not in control!" People working on self-irrelationship generally find it easier to understand how it works when they see irrelationship affecting how they relate to others.

Like her mother, Kathy is a compulsive caretaker. Her relationship with her mother mirrors her mother's caretaking relationship with everyone around her. But the wild card is the hair-trigger explosiveness her mom uses on her family if they don't show enough appreciation of her do-gooding. So what's the connection between—or, perhaps, explanation for—her so-called generosity outside the home and her volatility toward those who actually care about her the most?

"My mother never lets me love her. In our family, feelings are kept locked up tight. Oh, I know she cares about me. She cares about all of us. But it has to be 'at a distance.' And we have to accept that it has to be this way because if any of the rest of us show affection toward each other, she blows up and accuses us of not appreciating *her*."

Kathy's mom has the whole family brainlocked in an irrelationship double bind that ensures they stay isolated from one another. In time, Kathy began to feel compassion not just for her isolated mother, but for the isolated, unhappy child that she herself had been. As she came to understand the irrelationship dynamic, she began to step away from her own compulsive caretaking, directed first at her mother and then at others. Her relations with others redeveloped on the basis of genuine mutual appreciation and caring, but the indispensable foundation for this was her learning to understand and accept herself. This cleared space for her to share reciprocity and genuine caring with others and leave behind the anxiety-driven irrelationship routine that had controlled her life.

STAYING ON TARGET

Exercise
Discovery and Compassionate Empathy
Discovery reveals the hows and whys of irrelationship. The questions in the exercise below will help you discover specific instances of how irrelationship-driven mechanisms isolate you from yourself and others.

- What behaviors, such as caretaking, fixing, or rescuing, have I used to distract my attention from my anxious thoughts and feelings and my real needs?

- Have I or anyone else ever noticed how I divert my focus in this way? What was happening at the time? What did they say, and how did I respond?

- What other behaviors do I use in my interactions so I'll feel less anxious?

- How have my caretaking behaviors influenced my expectations concerning receiving caring or affection from others, or expectations of others withholding from or rejecting me?

- How have the exercises in this book changed how I view relationship expectations overall?

- In what ways has my caretaking gotten in the way of allowing myself to receive care from others? How has this prevented my awareness of my own feelings and needs?

- What impact has this book had on how I view self-acceptance?

Exercise
Blocking Reciprocity

The isolation created by irrelationship is the result of splitting off parts of myself, which leaves me unable to engage others or the world in a meaningful way. The healthy alternative is to become unconditionally accepting of my own history so I can develop safe relationships with others.

The following exercise explores ways of thinking and behaving that complicate reclaiming blocked-off parts of myself and my history.

1. Write down words and phrases you use on yourself that indicate self-blame for things that didn't go as you'd hoped, planned, or expected.

2. Recall and write down what you're feeling in those self-bashing moments, or when you recall those moments or experiences.

3. How do those words or phrases connect with the idea of self-protection explored in this book?

Exploring how you use negative ideas about yourself for self-protection is a vital piece of Discovery. The bullets below are some of the takeaways from this process:

- I've been trapped in an *irrelationship* process that prevents knowing and accepting myself—particularly my feelings, needs, and desires.

- The main reason I did this was to get away from anxiety that first began to develop when, as a small child, I didn't receive the caregiving I needed to feel safe.

- Use of irrelationship to escape anxiety typically goes on for years. In fact, by the time I'm an adult, it's so deeply ingrained that I can't recognize the crucial impact it has on how I see myself and the world—especially how it has kept me at a "safe" distance from others.

- This distance has resulted in all kinds of missed communication, including mistaken perceptions of my own denied feelings, which has worsened my estrangement from myself and others.

The following mindfulness exercise can promote the self-understanding created by the DREAM Sequence, and is recommended as a regular part of the practice:

- Set a timer for three to five minutes.

- Sit quietly in a comfortable seated position with feet flat on the floor. Tilt your head down slightly, with eyes partially open and looking at a spot a few feet in front of you, while focusing attention on your breathing.

- Take note of the thoughts that pass through your mind, then return your attention to your breathing.

- Allow yourself to be accepting of the various thoughts running through your head. This is an essential aspect of the practice of awareness. Attaching labels or judgment to them is a distraction that has no benefit for this practice, or your well-being.

- After the timer goes off, write down thoughts and feelings of any type that came up during the exercise. Consider each item or idea separately to see if they connect with any ideas you've gotten from using this book.

- Take the opportunity to focus on "lost" parts of yourself—ideas, feelings, or experiences that you believe you've unconsciously pushed aside by your irrelationship routine. Without judgment, look at those items and consider how they may impact how you view yourself and interact with others.

Sphere	What do I believe?	What am I discovering?	How does it feel?
How I feel in myself.			
How this affects the way I feel and act around family and friends.			
How this affects workplace relations.			

What does it mean?	What are the implications for myself in the future?	Ongoing Reflections

The next chapter explores the process of repairing my damaged relationship with myself and others by exposing the vulnerabilities I've hidden from myself.

CHAPTER TWELVE

Repair

The Repair step in the DREAM Sequence involves re-accessing split-off parts of myself to restore a whole relationship with who I really am, to enjoy a healthy interdependence[1] with others. This begins with reclaiming self-experiences that got lost when as a small child I reversed roles with my parent. This fuller experience of myself includes the reversal of the isolation and anxiety I suffered due to inadequate caretaking—feelings that didn't resolve later in life.

Psychologists use specific tools to gain insight into an individual's sense of clarity about who he or she is. The following scales are designed to elucidate core aspects of how we experience ourselves. This helps to identify gaps in identity and evoke important thoughts and feelings about oneself.

Self-Concept Clarity Scale	Sense-of-Self Scale
My beliefs about myself often contradict one another.	I wish I were more consistent in my feelings.
I might have a particular opinion of myself one day, and a different opinion on another day.	It's hard for me to figure out my own personality, interests, and opinions.
I spend a lot of time wondering what kind of person I really am.	I often think how fragile my existence is.
Sometimes I feel that I am not the person I appear to be.	I have a pretty good sense of what my long-term goals are.
When I reflect on the kind of person I've been in the past, I'm not sure what I was really like.	I sometimes wonder if people can actually see me.
I seldom experience conflict between different aspects of my personality.	Other people's thoughts and feelings carry greater weight with me than my own.
Sometimes I think I know other people better than I know myself.	I have a clear and definite sense of who I am and what I'm all about.
My beliefs about myself seem to change frequently.	It bothers me that my personality doesn't seem well defined.
If I were asked to describe my personality, my description would be different from one day to another.	I'm not sure that I can understand or put much trust in my thoughts and feelings.
I don't think I could tell someone what I'm really like.	"Who am I?" is a question I often ask myself.
In general, I have a clear sense of who I am and what I am.	I need other people to help me understand what I think or feel.
I sometimes have trouble making up my mind about things because I don't really know what I want.	I tend to be sure of myself and stick to my preferences, even when I'm around people with different preferences.

The Language of Conflict: The Real Trouble Comes out When the Fighting Stops

"I woke up one day and the storm was over," said Malik. "Or seemed to be. Mimi and I had worked through some pretty dark stuff—conflicts that came up again and again. Well one day, after it seemed like we'd gotten through the worst of it, I looked at her and asked myself, 'Now what?'"

Learning how to manage and work through conflict is an important part of relationships, especially intimate ones. For people bringing self-irrelationship into relationships, conflict can indicate inner irresolution, while also signaling a desire to keep communication open (Christiansen 2011; Metz 2018). By the same token, as Malik discovered, resolution of conflict can be unsettling, even frightening, because it leaves nowhere to hide.

"For me, that's when it hit the fan. When I suddenly wasn't on a mission to prove I was right and Mimi was wrong, I was left by myself with how messed up I felt inside—like I've felt since I was a kid. Then, outta nowhere, I came across the irrelationship book, and, for some reason, the title was like 'in my face'—*using dysfunction to hide from intimacy*! Well, I picked it up and read a little bit inside, and I knew my number had just been called. I'm not saying I 'got it.' But people in that book tell stories about how fighting was the only thing holding them together. Well I heard that. When Mimi and I stopped fighting, we suddenly—I don't know how to describe it. It was like there was this dead space between us. When we weren't fighting I didn't know how to even say anything to her." Malik shook his head. "I totally wasn't ready for that. It was damn lonely."

Almost from their first date, Malik "played the man" as Mimi's caretaker. And she liked it at first—like it was kind of romantic. But after they were married, it began to wear thin. She started resisting and resenting the way he was "managing" everything, "taking care of everything." Meanwhile, Malik thought all his caretaking was how a man is supposed to be toward a woman, so Mimi's resistance to it both angered and frightened him. Before they were married a year, this had become a slow burn for both of them that erupted into frequent arguments, which usually ended in a simmering stalemate they couldn't interpret or discuss. When they finally brought this situation into therapy, Malik managed to say that not looking after Mimi made him "feel dead inside," while Mimi had seriously begun to wonder "what Malik really thinks of me." Neither saw their fights as a covert way of trying to be *with* one another without risking the vulnerability of actually asking *for* each other. As their fighting increasingly gave way to silent stalemate, Malik, left without his caretaking irrelationship routine, rapidly hit an emotional bottom.

"Therapy was tough. First, figuring out that I actually missed fighting with Mimi, and then figuring out *why* I missed it—what a trip! And getting a grip on why she pushed back, and how each push made the other push back harder. But the hardest thing was admitting that if she didn't let me look after her the way I thought I should, that meant I couldn't be what a man's supposed to be, which basically meant I was nobody. And, well, thinking I'm nobody is real old stuff for me—going back to like when I was a little kid." Malik paused. "The thing was, 'feeling like I was nobody' was the *last* thing I could *ever* have admitted to Mimi. You don't do that. A man doesn't tell a woman—doesn't tell anybody, but especially his woman—that he's 'not all that,' or that he's scared of anything, or whatever. And I was scared all right. Being without Mimi scared me more than anything ever did in my whole life. The problem—well, another problem with that was, that Mimi's smart—real smart—and if I didn't keep up my act, she'd figure it *all* out. And then it would be game over because she'd know who I *really* am."

Why We Stay Unwell

"When I was growing up, my mom always used to say, 'Water seeks its own level'—like some kind of warning, or a philosophical thing. Well, looking back on all the stuff I've done to Stephanie, I don't believe it anymore."

Will was talking about how guilty and ashamed he felt because of the harm years of drug use and infidelity had caused his wife and their marriage. His mother's proverbial "wisdom," a passive-aggressive dig intended to say he deserved every bad thing that happened to him, was how she sidestepped the guilt she herself felt for Will's behavior.

As a "computer," the brain runs a variety of "developmental programs" that can imprint a child. Will's mother installed a corrupted operating system in Will early on, but it didn't originate with her: she'd taken it from her own family of origin—a socially transmitted disease, so to speak.

Stephanie had long ago given up asking Will to go back into rehab or to Narcotics Anonymous to try to get a handle on how his behavior had ruined their lives. So she was shocked when he reappeared after one of his drug-fueled disappearances and asked her if she would be willing to join him, not just in his working on getting clean, but on fixing what both had long felt was "missing from their relationship."

For Will and Stephanie to work through their painful history would require more from Stephanie than a conciliatory attitude toward Will. His drug use was fueled by his rejection of anything "human" about himself and of any kindness offered to him by others, including Stephanie. This blanket rejection included a refusal to examine how his abusive family history had affected him from childhood. Stephanie, meanwhile, unconsciously abetted Will's refusal, which allowed her to maintain distance between her image of herself and her actual feelings and needs.

The anxiety Stephanie felt in response to Will's destructive behavior was dwarfed by the anxiety and betrayal she felt when he suggested that they work together to fix their relationship. It was the most significant challenge they'd ever faced, both as individuals and as a couple. Could they agree to look unstintingly at the contributions each made to the distress in their relationship, for better and for worse? Were they willing to reconnect with the long-buried feelings they had for one another, and commit to rediscovering life *with* one another?

Self-Repair

Acknowledging fragmentation of my feelings and naming split-off parts of myself is essential to repair. Mapping out my identity with compassion for myself will, almost without my realizing it, bring about a healthy re-collection of myself, and restart development that was halted years ago as a result of childhood trauma. This unmasks the self-blame and shame underlying my self-numbing song-and-dance routine. Put more succinctly, reconnection with myself makes genuine connection with others possible.

STAYING ON TARGET

Exercise
Self-State Mapping

For this exercise, you'll need a notebook. Use steps one through five below to guide you as you fill out the table that follows. Retrieval of some items will take some time, so be patient. After reflection, write down what seems to correspond with what's being asked, without worrying about "getting it right." Whatever you write will tell you something worth knowing. Remember that the purpose of self-knowledge isn't to place blame, but to clear up what's going on.

Steps:

1. Identify different parts of yourself: Positive, Negative, Dissociated. Use the "Other" column for items that don't seem to fit in the first three. Do this for different parts of your life—intimate relationships, professional life, and so on.

2. For each item, ask yourself how it may connect with some aspect of your upbringing and family life when you were growing up. How do you think these aspects of your family life affect how you think and behave today?

3. Write down any additional thoughts that come to mind, even if they don't seem related.

4. If negative feelings about yourself begin to overwhelm you, pause to remember that blame is out of bounds and only confuses what you're trying to understand.

5. As you proceed, you may want to discuss some points with a person you trust. If you do that, write down what it was like to do that, and what the outcome was. Note that such outcomes sometimes develop over time, rather than popping out as a one-time "Aha!" moment.

The table is a guideline. Write as much as you feel the need to write. As more ideas emerge, feel free to go back to earlier parts and change or add to them.

Sphere	Positive	Negative	Dissociated	Other
How I feel in myself.				
How this affects the way I feel and act around family and friends.				
How this affects workplace relations.				

Developmental Impact	Thoughts	Feelings	Ongoing Reflections

Exercise

Recurring Issues that Prevent Problem-Solving

Repair requires feeling safe, which is why finger-pointing is out of bounds when doing the 40-20-40. This applies as much to myself as to others when asking how my part in relationship issues get in the way of figuring out solutions.

Identify an ongoing, troublesome issue in one of your relationships. It can be something as simple as always being late for coffee dates or as complicated as anxiety around your sex life. For purposes of the exercise, the type of relationship doesn't matter. Credit yourself with "extra points" if the issue is one you deliberately avoid thinking about.

- Imagine discussing the issue with the other person involved. Take note of any possible overlap in how you think the two of you might see the issue.

- Apply the 40-20-40 model (see below) to the issue.

You	Midpoint	The Other
0 Feet	5 Feet	10 Feet
0 percent	50 percent	100 percent

- Next, imagine widening the line in the middle of the table to 20 percent of the table's width, leaving 40 percent on either side.

You	Expanded Middle			Me
0 Feet	4 Feet		6 Feet	10 Feet
	40 percent	20 percent	40 percent	

- Perform a 40-20-40 assessment answering the following questions about the identified issue:

1. What do you think this issue is *really* about? (Is one party avoiding doing something because they just don't like doing it? What underlying issues may be involved? Do you feel your partner should give you a "pass" because of how generous you are in other ways? Or vice versa?)

2. Why do you think this issue should be addressed, rather than just "letting it ride?"

3. How does it impact other parts of your relationship? Relationships with others?

4. What are the benefits of leaving it unresolved, that is, by taking either too little (less than 40 percent) or too much accountability (more than 60 percent) for the issue?

5. How could you start resolving the issue by breaking it up into smaller, manageable parts, and working toward meeting in the "20 percent middle" of shared accountability?

6. How does breaking the issue up this way affect how you perceive the issue and your willingness to resolve it?

Repair Takeaway Points:

- Self-Interactive Repair helps me to see how irrelationship has affected me as an individual.

- Repair of my relationship with me overcomes resistance to being up-front about my feelings—a giant step in reconnecting with pushed-away parts of myself.

- Self-Interactive Repair allows me to engage all of me in a process of problem-solving.

- Self-Interactive Repair demonstrates that the way things have always been isn't the way they always have to be.

- Holding on to the idea of "blame" is unhelpful and distorts reality.

Now let's return to the mindfulness exercise introduced in the previous chapter. It's been tweaked here to complement the interactive repair process. Remember that nonjudgmental observation of my own thoughts and feelings is vital to moving forward in a healthy way.

- Set a timer and sit comfortably and quietly with attention on the breath.

- Take note of the thoughts that pass through your mind, then return your attention to your breath.

- As often as necessary, remind yourself that ideas of "good or bad" or "right or wrong" are out of place. The purpose of the exercise is to become familiar with my thoughts and impulses and the things that make me uneasy.

- After the timer signals, make notes about positive and negative ideas about interactive repair that came up in the quiet.

CHAPTER THIRTEEN

Empowerment

An empowered relationship with myself depends on developing and using self-awareness. How is this done? The 40-20-40, combined with the fine-grained self-awareness developed by Self-State Mapping, can initiate and mediate healing self-integration. Three processes are involved: 1) specific self-awareness of both the difficult and the attractive parts of myself, 2) self-bonding through self-directed compassionate empathy, and 3) open internal communication that nurtures dialogue with myself. Working together, these synergize self-organization, which impels progress toward a preferred, more adaptive long-term trajectory. Empowerment, therefore, connects me with myself and a broad experience of others and solidifies the process begun in the Discovery and Repair stages.

A child's capacity to accept and enjoy solitude, rather than experience it as empty loneliness, depends on her ability to integrate her primary caregiver's comforting, loving presence. This models and enables the caring self-partnering discussed earlier and matures into the ability to regulate anxiety and accept the world as she finds it—capacities fundamental to intimacy with self and with others.

40-20-40-Based Empowerment as a Way of Life

"The end point of years of cold war was a terrible loneliness," said Joan. "We were so isolated from each other. We were quietly driving each other crazy, even though, or *because* everything about our lives was set up so that we didn't connect. The hard part of figuring this out was that it came from how each of us dealt with ourselves! There was no such thing as 'me time.' Solitude was out of bounds. So we were desperately demanding something from each other that nobody can actually give another person. In a way, we *looked* like we were joined at the hip, but really we were just handcuffed to each other. You just can't get self-love from somebody else, any more than somebody else can take your selfie!"

The 40-20-40 space is threateningly transformative, which makes it empowering. When the self-irrelationship routine breaks down, empowerment requires use of the full depth of myself to acquire self-knowledge, making me able to experience others. This is done by imagining ourselves in interaction with someone about whom we feel conflicted, as Joan did when she imagined using the 40-20-40 with her wife, Teresa.

"When I first visualized the '20' of the 40-20-40 as a space between us where we work out giving and taking in equal shares, it felt bizarre at first—totally alien. I've always been the doer, the one who had to get the attention of others—my parents and friends, girlfriends, and now even my wife. I literally don't know how to 'be' if I *don't* operate that way."

Joan was willing, with reservations, to ask Teresa to try out the process with her, though she had approximately zero hope Teresa would agree. But she did agree—so quickly that it almost shocked Joan. They tried (with some rough first attempts, which is usual with practically everybody) giving each other a few minutes to each talk about her own contribution to how things felt in their marriage, both good and bad. Finger-pointing, blame, or back talk is out of bounds. The partner who isn't speaking listens, which usually takes practice. They take as many turns at timed sharing and listening as they choose. Often, a recurrent everyday household issue will lead to some of the most profound experiences of listening and learning about one another.

"When it comes to relationships, I've always sat back and let others do the heavy lifting," admitted Teresa. "When I was growing up, my mom and dad were constantly 'looking out for me,' which was just their way of forcing what they wanted on me. But I was a little rebel inside. I always acted the 'good girl' and seemed to do what they wanted. But I never really told them what I wanted or thought about anything. It was actually kind of passive-aggressive, and it drove them crazy. So they just got more and more controlling, but I never seemed to respond one way or the other. It really made them writhe, because I wasn't outwardly rebellious or meek and submissive. Well, I just let them go on and on, whatever. By the time I went to college I was getting a weird kind of pleasure from it. Kinda sadistic, huh? Well, when I started having girlfriends, I know I seemed like somebody who could easily be controlled, but it wasn't like that. I just kept aloof and didn't really give any feedback one way or the other when somebody tried to control me, same as with my mom and dad. It was a very underhanded way of keeping myself from getting pushed around."

It was scary for Joan when she asked Teresa to try the 40-20-40. But Teresa was really in love with her, and Joan's withholding routine was growing threadbare and uncomfortable. So she said yes without really being sure why. As it turned out, that unsureness was all that was needed. The 40-20-40 typically undercuts defenses and exposes irrelationship routines, which pretty quickly leads to reencounter with dissociated feelings. If we stay with the 40-20-40, insight into how we've been living our lives comes into view. Owning the truth about this part of "me" makes the anxiety connected with it fade away. This by itself is the basic mechanism of empowerment.

"So," Teresa continued, "we tried it. Some fits and starts at first, and it felt kind of mechanical, but I think that may even have made it less scary. I think it was the first time ever that we just sat and listened to each other. I mean, I listened to her without telling myself how full of crap she was."

Joan picked up on Teresa's burgeoning openness. "Almost from the start, I saw something different happening inside Teresa's head. I don't even know if she was aware of it. But it was like seeing her naked for the first time—exciting as hell, but what if—what *if?* What if she takes off as soon as she 'sees me'?"

Joan and Teresa found themselves "meeting in the middle" of anxiety and negotiation faster than a lot of couples do. Each was frightened of what the other would *really* think of her when they dropped the self-distancing they'd used for years. This is the real threat of intimacy: revealing empathy and emotional investment, which add up to vulnerability to one another.

As can be seen from Joan and Teresa's experience, going forward despite anxiety allows me to:

1. Experience lost parts of myself, which allows me to interact voluntarily with others and establish connection.

2. Understand how my contribution affects my interactions with others—both functional and dysfunctional.

3. Tolerate higher levels of anxiety than when I'm disconnected from my feelings.

4. Understand how the way I interact now is influenced by interactions from the past—especially interactions in my family of origin.

5. Feel dissociated experiences that got in the way of my experiencing the world as it actually is. This expands options available to me in my life now.

6. Use these insights to re-view stultifying irrelationship patterns with others.

"Doing *something* together" is exactly what self-irrelationship is designed to prevent. Its opposite is empowerment—openness to connection *to* someone *with* that someone, both the "good" and the "bad," without having to control flow or outcome.

"Insisting on isolating to feel safe got me nothing and nowhere," Teresa put in. "And that was my doing and nobody else's. The last thing I thought would actually *make* me feel safe was telling somebody that I felt *un*safe—especially Joan."

Joan agreed. "The funny thing is I was hiding in almost the same place. I accepted what I got back from you as 'okay,' which of course it wasn't. But I told myself I was happy with it; I still drove you crazy trying to get more—trying to get you to show me just a little more Teresa."

Showing ourselves to one another feels like a gamble when we're not used it. Usually, though, remembering why we were so crazy about each other in the first place, and letting each other see that, tees up a new shot at the intimacy that seemed so scary before. And doing it together makes it a completely different game.

STAYING ON TARGET

Exercise

Expanding Empowerment

Embracing and dialoguing with locked-away parts of myself builds empowerment, which almost automatically opens me to a sense of connection with others. Having seen how the 40-20-40 promotes this process, use the following questions to gain insight into how your song-and-dance routine keeps you isolated from your own feelings and needs.

- What would it feel and look like to accept unconditionally the cutoff parts of myself that I keep distant with a song-and-dance routine?

- What is it like to consider using disturbing parts of my history and my feelings about them as a tool for creating a better connection with the world?

- What would it feel like to accept and embrace fully what I need, feel, and want, and to say "yes" to those parts of me?

- How would this be empowering?

- How does it feel to imagine a relationship with another person in which what each wants and needs carries equal weight, and over which I have no control?

- What would it feel like to choose such a relationship deliberately?

- How could self-empowerment play a role in restoring relationships disrupted by my controlling song-and-dance routines?

- How would openness and honesty about my feelings and needs change how I build relationships with others?

Now let's return to the mindfulness exercise, this time with an eye to the Empowerment step of the DREAM Sequence. Remember to practice nonjudgmental observation of your thoughts, feelings, and experience of self.

- Set a timer as before. In a comfortable seated position, sit quietly with attention on the breath.

- Note the stream of thoughts passing through your mind, and then return your attention to your breath.

- As often as necessary, remind yourself that this practice has no right/wrong or good/bad: its purpose is to learn about our thoughts, impulses, and the things we are uneasy about or resist.

- After the allotted time, make notes about how the idea of empowerment affects you positively and negatively.

Repeat the Self-Mapping Exercise from Chapter Twelve with an eye toward the Empowerment Step.

CHAPTER FOURTEEN

Alternatives: Expanding my Choices about Who I Am and How I Live

"People can learn to control and change their behavior," says van der Kolk (2014, 351), "but only if they feel safe enough to experiment with new solutions." Compassionate empathy makes space for alternative experiences of ourselves—and breaks us out of the isolation of our long-term vigilant maintenance of the defensive split between self and other—as we interact with lost parts of ourselves and create new ways to relate to others, starting with those closest to us, and extending to all areas of our lives. Self-mutuality improves intimacy with close others, but also extends empowerment into friendship, professional relationships, and everyday living.

Early Intervention/Prevention

"I can't believe you're treating your sister like that!" Lily's father shouted.

Mike felt angry and strangely sad when he saw Lily pulling a whale-shaped spoon out of Suzy's hand and pushing her away, nearly making her fall. He was also surprised at how quickly his anger boiled over. He was insightful enough to surmise that it had something to do with disappointments from his own childhood—painful memories of rage from his mother and the unexplained disappearance of his father—but he had buried most of the specifics of those experiences so deeply that he was scarcely able to recall them. Moreover, their incompatibility with how he viewed himself in the here and now had long ago made him choose unconsciously to keep them unremembered. As a result, unaccustomed feelings of vulnerability and rage sometimes surfaced that seemed out of proportion to the events triggering them.

"Time OUT!" he yelled, marching Lily down the hall to her bedroom. He remembered at the last second not to slam the door—a particularly provocative action in their household.

Suzy's attention-seeking and rapid-fire demands had been a trial to the whole family that day. Lily usually went along with her sister's age-appropriate behavior pretty cheerfully, but on this particular day, both she and her father snapped.

Mike and his wife Hannah are professionals with their own businesses. Since the birth of Lily, they'd taken pains to arrange work and free time to allow for shared family activities while also giving each parent individual time with the girls. But it wasn't always easy. Shortly after Lily was born, Hannah was diagnosed with a life-threatening illness whose treatment required periods of isolation from her family. Mike accommodated this by rearranging his personal and professional life to maintain a stable family pattern. Hannah's recovery led to their deciding to have a second child, whom Lily welcomed from the start, and usually treated with love and patience.

In response to the Lily's impatient reaction to Suzy, Mike gave Lily a five-minute time-out, but after only about two minutes she came out of her bedroom full of tears. Mike's initial impulse to send her back to her room was stopped by the look on Lily's face as she ran to Suzy and took her in her arms with wailing apologies, promising "I'll be a better sister," and "I'll try not to be so selfish." Then, looking at Mike, she said, "I'm sorry—I forgot she's just a baby!"

A sweet but deep sadness welled up inside Mike as he recalled times that Lily had reproached him with "Daddy, I'm just a kid" when he lost patience with her. Both of them, he realized, had to learn to let others be who they are, which at this moment meant letting his seven-year-old be a seven-year-old.

What Mike didn't yet fully see was how certain dynamics between himself and his wife and children resonated with what he had experienced as a child. Put another way, he was unconsciously projecting his "inner family system" on the present without fully connecting the painful sadness that welled up in him upon reflection about his daughter with leftover grief for his own childhood losses and disappointment.

Mike apologized and hugged both his daughters, but he remained uneasy. When would he lose his temper again? He knew something unnamed inside himself remained unresolved.

No More Sky Legs

Most nights after their Netflix binge, Meg would ask Richie for a hug, which he usually deflected with the type of cat-and-mouse game practiced by many people who avoid physical affection. Meg sometimes playacted "adult passion" by putting her legs in the air, which they jokingly called her "sky legs." Ultimately, however, their dance around intimacy and sexual connection reinforced the space between them.

After their second child was born, Meg and Richie had increasing difficulty creating space for intimacy amid the ongoing demands of family and professional life. And, while play is a vital part of intimate connection, Richie's cat-and-mouse game or his tickling her till she begged for mercy were actually sending her the unconscious message that showing care directly made him uneasy;

it only left Meg wondering if the message was that Richie had lost interest in her.

When interviewed, both believed themselves to be doing the majority of the caretaking in the relationship, but at the same time each felt reluctant to accept the care offered by the other. In other words, they were caught in a self-sufficiency song-and-dance routine while denying their own desires and needs—including the emotional connection and intimacy they both missed and longed for. Nevertheless, this longstanding unspoken agreement between them was breached when Meg tentatively asked for her post-Netflix hug. Once in therapy, Richie and Meg began—a little bit at a time— to see how talking honestly to each other about their anxiety and reluctance was precisely the tool needed to transition them into interactive repair.

"Who knows?" Richie said one day. "Maybe no more sky legs?"

Meg missed a beat, then smiled mischievously. "Hmm . . . Maybe not!"

STAYING ON TARGET

Constructive Alternatives vs. Mutually Assured Destruction

I make my crazy work for me by facing head-on the part of me I have pushed out of my consciousness. When I learn to accept that part of myself, I begin to make space for alternatives—new ways of building and being in relationships that allow for development of authentic mutuality.

The following exercise helps expose pitfalls I'm likely to experience when learning to communicate and share vulnerability. The exercise will also help me spot opportunities for collaboration that lead to the hospitable connections with others I would historically thwart with my habitual isolation.

The exercise examines how disagreements with others in my life today turn into episodic arguments, infliction of pain, and retaliation, and then, returning the focus onto myself, looks for *my part* in whatever's going wrong. Developing this skill then becomes an early warning system that can prompt me to make better choices in how I participate in conflict—or even to avert it. With practice, this dramatically changes how I view myself and virtually any human interaction.

Looking at ongoing disagreements —historic and current—with others, identify and write down recurring patterns you see, and the feelings that go with them. Some of these will be easy to spot, but others will probably require reflection, and perhaps more honesty than you want to bring to it.

Using the schema below, write down alternative behaviors or strategies you could have used in those conflicts which may have led to a more satisfying outcome for you, as well as for the others involved.

1. Problematic Pattern or Behavior:

    _____

    _____

    _____

    Alternative 1. _____

    Alternative 2. _____

    Alternative 3. _____

2. Problematic Pattern or Behavior:

_____

_____

_____

Alternative 1. _____

Alternative 2. _____

Alternative 3. _____

Next, return to an issue that you can identify from the Repair and the Empowerment stages of the DREAM Sequence.

In the table below, trace your process and the progress made as you worked on resolving the issue.

- The Issue_____

How has my perception of the causes of this issue changed?	
Whom has it harmed and how?	
How have I justified or ignored my part in the harm?	
How do I feel about the harm?	
How does it feel to repair or consider repairing such a situation?	
How does it feel to step aside or consider stepping aside from isolating and destructive behavior?	
What advice would I give others to avoid similar situations?	

When ready, proceed to the next set of questions.

How has this issue affected my relationship with my partner?	
What specific harm has it caused?	
How can the harm be used to create a different way of relating?	
How can past harms be used to take better care of the relationship that we share?	
What feelings do each of us have about learning practical new ways of taking care of our relationship?	
What guidelines can we use to help us sustain new ways of addressing relationship issues?	

Interactive repair is a setup for empowerment, both in myself and as shared with others. It comes about through the deliberate practice of hearing and understanding lost, dissociated parts of myself. Its bottom line is relationship sanity.

The following exercise builds on work done in previous chapters but expands it into a practice of creating alternatives for managing the hard parts of relationships.

Take time to reflect, and then write down your responses to the following:

- What is it like to consider that I don't have to handle conflict the way I've done in the past?

- What could alternative solutions look like in day-to-day conflicts?

- What impact could such an alternative have on how I see myself and others?

- What is my reaction to the idea of replacing arguing with creative problem-solving?

- Imagine a 40-20-40 conversation with blocked-off parts of yourself—the parts you don't want to think about. Imagine speaking frankly about what you've learned from these exercises about how you handle conflict.

Exercise
Developing Alternatives through Compassionate Empathy
Recall a situation in which someone wronged you without causing serious harm.

- What feelings come up for you when you consider viewing that person with empathy?

- What do you think could happen if you put aside your victim role and the resentment that goes with it?

- What connection do you see between self-acceptance and attempting to extend empathy to others?

- What connections do you see between self-acceptance, empathy, and intimacy?

Exercise

Compassionate Empathy as Catalyst of Alternatives

- Sit quietly and, remembering that you are safe with yourself, allow yourself to recall the vulnerability you feel when recalling negative experiences from your past.

- Expand the idea of safety to include the world in which you live every day: other people, your neighborhood, workplace, and anywhere else you encounter others.

- Consider the possibility that the new openness and excitement you're experiencing within yourself can be part of your connection with anyone around you.

- Imagine this newly discovered and growing part of yourself as an actual space for sharing unconditional hospitality and compassionate empathy for lost parts of yourself.

- Visualize the lost parts of yourself that you're reclaiming. Imagine them as part of the complete "you" in interaction with others, including the feelings of vulnerability this arouses. Reflect on how this could change your experience of closeness—intimacy—with others.

Reflection on Empowerment

Return to the practice of observing your thoughts, this time to gauge the impact, conscious or not, of the idea of creating alternatives. Observing our thoughts as nonjudgmental spectators doesn't come easy to many of us. But with practice, you'll become accustomed to accessing information you've kept at a distance, enabling better choices.

- Set a timer and, as before, sit quietly, focusing on your breath. Notice where you feel it most readily, usually at the nostrils or for some people in the rising and falling of the chest or abdomen. Allow your attention to rest there.

- Be lightly aware of the stream of thoughts and feelings passing through your mind and then return your attention to your breath. When you notice your thoughts wandering, return your attention with good humor to the sensation of your breath.

- Remain nonjudgmental to the extent possible about your performance. It is expected that your thoughts will wander, and your attention will waver away from simply noticing your breath. This is part of the practice. If you become anxious about whether you are doing a "good job" or "the right way," take note of that, and bring your attention gently back to the breath.

- Following this practice, take notes about your thoughts, your reactions to them, and what doing this practice is like for you.

CHAPTER FIFTEEN

Mutuality with Myself

Mutuality is where crazy works for us on all cylinders. Bessel van der Kolk (2014, 81) says that in mental health, "the critical issue is reciprocity: being truly heard and seen by the people around us, feeling that we are held in someone else's mind and heart." Mutuality's converse—irrelationship—stunts playfulness and diverts growth, resilience, and flexibility, not just in childhood but across the lifespan.

In the *Phase-Oriented Treatment of Structural Dissociation* model (Steele, van der Hart & Nijenhuis, 2005), which seeks to repair structural splits within the personality, the final phase of treatment is *Integration and Rehabilitation*, and includes the following tasks:

- Overcoming the phobia of normal life.
- Overcoming the phobia of healthy risk-taking and change.
- Overcoming the phobia of intimacy.

Psychoanalyst Daniel Shaw (2014, *xv*) says that "(w)hat is developmentally traumatic is the . . . caregiver's rejection of the child's subjectivity, and the caregiver's refusal to allow intersubjective recognition to be mutual." Intersubjectivity is a state of relationship in which each person can recognize and accept the other's independent, valid perspective (subjectivity) without needing to necessarily agree or disagree, in mutually respectful co-presence. It opens up major avenues for communication and relatedness which people trapped in irrelationship cannot easily fathom.

Mutuality reassociates the self–self and self–other experiences that were self-protectively split off during development and replaced with compulsive caretaking routines. Achieving the intersubjective relatedness with oneself that accommodates conflicting and formerly mutually exclusive narcissistic cores adds the depth and complexity necessary for the personality to enjoy solitude as well as time with others. This reunion of the self–self and self–other ("relationship sanity") is achieved through compassionate empathy for oneself.

When we make mistakes—even big ones—that jeopardize connections, relationship sanity provides a means of figuring out what went wrong and how to fix it, and going forward without fear of being punished forever. This can be complicated; how we live our lives is often messy, and movement forward may require that I compromise my personal comfort for a time.

The phases of dependence in relationships, as identified by Carnes, Laaser, and Laaser (1999), suggest that we develop a sense of identity by passing through phases of dependency; that is, our experience teaches us how much we can make depending on others part of our lives:

1. **Dependence:** We need and want help.

2. **Counterdependence:** We need help but resist it.

3. **Independence:** We're self-sufficient and don't need help.

4. **Interdependence:** We're able to give and receive help.

Consistent with Carnes, Laaser, and Laaser's model, interdependence *within oneself* is synergized by interdependence with others and vice versa. Irrelationship, then, is its opposite. Investment in irrelationship is stepping away from relationship sanity to act out intimacy-related anxiety through enactment of GRAFTS behaviors. We can identify ways in which we use GRAFTS on ourselves; for example, when I try to act Good to convince myself that I *am* Good, and then encounter parts of myself that I think are Bad, my sense of myself crashes and I panic.

Mutual acceptance is built on compassionate empathy and allows balanced give and take, including in the areas of love and caregiving. Mutuality among parts of myself, therefore, is the hallmark of relationship sanity that welcomes whole experience of myself. As noted earlier, the 40-20-40 (or "self–other assessment") is useful for achieving this relationship *with me*.

Healthy Dependency?

Dependency is often viewed as a negative trait, and can certainly be destructive. However, this limited and limiting viewpoint is only a half-truth concerning the nature of our humanity. For many, the approach of the winter holidays brings isolation or fear of isolation to the forefront of our consciousness. As a remedy, we often turn to relationships loaded with irrelationship-based defense routines to relieve the immediate fear of being alone, but which end up adding to the sense of isolation characterizing our lives and histories.

What is meant by *healthy* reliance on others? If the idea raises feelings of unease, this may be a marker of ambivalence about closeness, including about sharing empathy and a sense of my own vulnerability. However, dependency can be "depathologized" (Bornstein 1998) so that we permit ourselves the quintessentially human need and desire to access and share our own unique human experience, for better and for worse, and not just to relieve stress but to build connection. Without such connection, meaningful relationships of any kind can't develop. Moreover, the fact is that our experiences include many examples of mutual dependency that add to the richness and complexity of living. We are part of groups: teams, families, and religious, community, and political organizations whose impact is felt within and outside themselves.

Vital to their functioning is a group focus on agreed-upon goals and the interdependence of its members in working toward their shared purpose. Without such interdependence we could achieve no political, scientific, or social aims, and would scarcely be functional in any meaningful sense. Instead, we'd be living in the fantasy of total self-sufficiency described earlier. By contrast, healthy dependence allows us to coexist effectively and rediscover ourselves in the context of relationships that are resilient, supportive, and open to spontaneity (Iacoviello and Charney 2014).

Relationship researcher Sue Johnson (2103, 21–22) has written that "(e)motional dependency is not immature or pathological; it is our greatest strength . . . Far from being a sign of frailty, strong emotional connection is a sign of mental health. It is emotional isolation that is the killer. The surest way to destroy people is to deny them loving human contact."

Reciprocity and Reawakening the Creation of Health

Reciprocity is the foundation for emotional health and well-being and is associated with empowerment and psychological resilience (Southwick and Charney 2012).[1] Research shows what common sense tells us: healthy social relationships are reciprocal, with good self-esteem across the lifespan . . . "[T]he link between people's social relationships and their level of self-esteem is truly reciprocal in all developmental stages across the life span, reflecting a positive feedback loop between the constructs" (Harris and Orth 2019).

Now, how about self-reciprocity? Can I form a nurturing ecosystem within my own psyche? When I approach myself with compassion, the craziness resulting from rejection of competing, unrecognized desires and needs within myself can give way to a joyful, creative relationship with my craziness that's at peace with realistic expectations of others and the world. This allows for the healthy developmental environment we were denied as small children, and ultimately leads to healthy self-relationship.

The Moment of Self-Recognition

An undeniable strength of those affected by irrelationship is the adaptability that dysfunctional caregivers forced them to develop. In cases of full-blown post-traumatic stress disorder, this may cross into near-hypervigilance as a survival skill, to be optimally prepared when crises develop. Adults with this background are well prepared for some situations, but woefully unprepared for others.

When Barbara started treatment, she wasn't convinced that anything was wrong with her life, although she admitted to the vague feeling that something just "wasn't quite right" in herself and her relations with others. Her skepticism quickly turned to astonishment when she first heard the term "irrelationship," which she said was "what I've been living with all my life!" As therapy proceeded, she realized that she was starting a conversation with herself that she "had never come close to imagining."

"I've always had mixed feelings about myself as a mother," she continued, "wondering whether what I gave my daughters was ever 'good enough,' or what they even needed in life. I always felt it was important for them to see themselves in a loving way, and as part of a larger living environment. I've always known how important it is to be comfortable in the world and able to love and to feel loved. So far so good.

"But they also learned something else from me that I didn't realize at the time. In their preschool years, I started going through a depression that lasted for years. Before long, I started feeling really guilty because I just couldn't take care of my girls, which made my depression even worse. To this day, I've got big blank spaces in my memory of those years.

"One thing I *do* remember, though, is the scared look on my girls' faces, standing next to my bed, trying to get me to eat and drink things they'd bring me. They'd be saying 'You'll get better, Mommy' or 'It'll be okay, Mommy.' Oh my God, how that tore at me! Later on, I realized they weren't just trying to encourage me, they were *pleading* with me to get better. So, in a way, I'm not even sure which is worse—remembering it or not remembering. The point is, those two little girls were doing for me what I should have been doing for them. *They* were looking after *me*! They were being *mommy*!

"Once, when my depression landed me in the hospital, Tillie, my younger girl, sneaked her kitten into the hospital—she knew I loved cats, of course—to try to help me remember the good parts of life at home so that I'd come back to them. My other daughter Jessie loved hugging and was really good at it. We loved gardening together. Well one day when I was really manic, we were out in the back gardening when I got it into my head that if we could knock down part of the kitchen, we could make room for more garden. It was just crazy. Well, my little Jessie didn't answer right away, but then after a little bit she said, 'I don't think making a bigger garden is really such a good idea, Mom.' Look who was acting like a mommy!

"Another part of this that I've figured out is that, since I was a kid, I always *had* to show everybody what a good girl I was. And as I got older, that didn't stop. I was always on the lookout for people around me going through something bad, so I could find a way to work myself into their situation so I could fix it or something. It sounds altruistic in a way, but it turns out that's not really what it was about at all. You see, I grew up in a family that always left me to myself, even when something had really upset me. So I figured out early on that not only was I on my own, but I was expected to be the perfect child who never needed anything from anybody.

"Later, to get away from how isolated and lonely that felt, I was always looking for people who were having some kind of problems so I could inject myself into their lives. That way I got to be the hero while at the same time getting away from the loneliness I felt all the time.

"Well, I know now that the depression I went through when the girls were small was 'leftover' from trying to outrun or outthink my feelings, like you said! And my poor baby girls got to see what it looked like when I just couldn't run anymore.

"It took a while for me to 'get it,' though—this connection between what I'd been through as a kid and, well, my disconnection from what was happening *now*. I think what I probably always told myself was that the best thing I could do about my childhood was leave it behind, and later, make sure what happened to me didn't happen to my girls. But making a conscious choice to do that didn't undo the damage. All that old pain in the background literally kept me unable to engage with myself or anybody else.

"What really surprised me, though, was that when I finally let myself just *start* to remember what being a kid was like for me, it was like a door opened—not just inside me, but between me and my girls. And what's funny is, when that door started opening, Tillie and Jessie seemed to sense that something different was going on with me almost right away. And what a change it's made! Just being able to talk about being scared or worried about something with each other has made what it's like for us to be together almost a miracle. For me, I was able to feel *all kinds* of feelings that I used to push away—not only sadness and fear, but also joy and gratitude. It's not always a cakewalk, but I feel way better, way more complete. Still so much to learn, but now I'm actually excited about the future instead of afraid of, well, everything.

"Another piece of this is that feeling I had to be everybody's 'good guy' seems to have gone on a long vacation, thank God. Don't get me wrong, I definitely still believe in being 'there' for others, and I've tried to teach that to my girls, but life just feels so different when I don't need to be anybody's hero—not even Tillie and Jessie's. Seems like I can just take the world as it comes, whatever that is."

STAYING ON TARGET

Exercise

Interdependence and Relationship Sanity

To break with irrelationship and build relationship sanity requires that I figure out why I first started refusing to depend on others. The following exercise examines my relationships with those who, in both their presence and their absence, had the greatest impact on me as a child. Either can drive my willingness or reluctance to reveal my needs and vulnerability.

Below is a typical list of important players in a child's life. Next to each, make notes as follows:

- How you think each may have affected your willingness to let others see your feelings, especially negative feelings such as anger or sadness.

- Include memories of how each person reacted when you made mistakes or did something "wrong." Were they helpful and supportive, or critical and annoyed? Did they help you understand "mistakes," or did they just make you feel bad? Try to include specific experiences and describe your feelings about them, then and now.

- Finally, for each person below, write a brief notation on the impact you think those past interactions still have on you today. The list is generic, so add anyone with whom you can remember significant interactions.

  » Parents/Primary Caregivers

  » Siblings/Other Family Members

  » Teachers

  » Friends

  » Employers and Coworkers

  » Other Adults (specify)

Clarifying how I feel about welcoming back my "cutoff" parts is vital to building relationship sanity. The following exercise will help.

Exercise
Attitudes toward Caring for and about Myself
Caregiving transactions generally fall into the following categories:

- **Quid pro quo**: Care provided with the implicit or explicit understanding that the giver is entitled to expect something back.

- **Non-emotionally-involved care:** Care that does not involve personal connection, such as that provided by professional caregivers, between persons who know one another without emotional connection, or between strangers.

- **Care as a means of control with unbalanced personal investment:** Caretaking as a one-way transaction with little or no concern for the actual needs of the target of the behavior.

- **Minimal care:** Caretaking, sometimes impersonal, administered out of a sense of obligation; may be accompanied by feelings of guilt, resentment, or other negative emotions; target of caretaking experiences little or no benefit, and may be unaware it's occurring.

- **Accepting care:** Caregiver and recipient authentically and unconditionally accept their respective roles vis-à-vis one another, but are open to changes in their roles.

The following exercise may help develop insight into why you accept or reject needed assistance from those around you.

1. Describe an experience of caregiving that involved you as giver or receiver. Don't worry about whether or not your scenario seems to correspond to any of the classifications above.

2. Many of us have experienced caregiving that has interfered with our ability to accept care and services we need. This can range from care needed during convalescence from illness, to

emotional support during a life crisis, to needing government services after losing a job. Write a brief description of an experience in which you needed support from other people or from a service agency. What led to your needing such support? What was it like for you to be in that position?

3. Look back over your life, especially early childhood, and write about experiences with significant caregivers:

    - What personal qualities do you recall that had an impact on what it was like for you to have them taking care of you?

    - Describe an experience where the manner in which care was offered to you made you hesitant or uneasy about accepting it.

4. Think about a caregiving experience with someone who is part of your life now. It may be a significant other, a healthcare professional, a neighbor, or even a casual acquaintance who did something nice for you. What personal qualities did that person bring to the interaction, and how did the encounter make you feel? Now think about someone in your life whom you feel accepts you as you are. What qualities in that person affect how you experience their caring?

5. Return to an issue that you identified while doing the DREAM Sequence. Refilter that issue through the lens of Mutuality. Imagine what it would be like to process the issue reciprocally with a person with whom you are connected and think you could trust, or would like to.

- The Issue_____

Compare how you view the issue now with how you viewed it when you first picked up this book.	
· How does reclaiming your own needs and desires change how you see the issue?	
· How does that change how you view your part in issues in other parts of your life?	
Comment on this statement: Unconditional openness to what I bring to the table improves my relationship with myself and how I solve problems.	
Unconditional acceptance of myself changes what it's like to think about connection with and dependence on others.	

Describe or comment on each bullet: · Changing feelings about the identified issue.	
· Changes in how I view myself and others. *(Focus especially on the idea of isolation.)*	
What practical things can I do to build mutuality into my everyday life?	

Exercise
Mutuality

- Reflect on what it's like to work through a long-standing issue in isolation while insisting that you're self-sufficient.

- How does improved acceptance of yourself and your history affect how you think about and solve problems?

- As in the previous steps, set the timer and relax in a seated position, bringing your attention to your breath, while observing the stream of thoughts passing through your mind. Then refocus on your breath.

- Remember that the aim of this practice is to become aware of what your mind does, and to practice stepping back from it without judgment.

- Write down your thoughts, feelings, and insights, including the uncomfortable ones.

- A self 40-20-40 based on Mutuality as a problem-solving practice may be useful.

Letting Your Crazy Work For You

"People create the reality they need
in order to discover themselves."

ERNEST BECKER, *THE DENIAL OF DEATH*

The good news is that you're getting back your relationship with yourself. The hard part is that this comes with reawakened awareness of the feelings that went missing when you lost that relationship. As with any part of life, some days will be easier than others, but that was true before you started getting yourself back.

Users quickly find that the DREAM Sequence isn't a linear, sequential process. Instead, each of its steps are doors that remain open for ongoing discovery, processing, integration, and growth, so that satisfaction with your life continues to build and change in exciting and unexpected ways that arrest and reverse the vicious circle of irrelationship. As you become accustomed to its momentum, you won't need encouragement to stay with the process. Its pleasure will become self-sustaining.

For many of us, the idea of finding the right mate and falling in love is an essential marker of self-realization. Self-irrelationship short-circuits romantic and any other type of connection with others by confining me to the dead space I've spent years both building and avoiding. As long as what's at the other side of that dead space remains unknown and unaddressed, my self-irrelationship song-and-dance routine will prevent connection with others, even in cases of encounters that seem to suggest a real possibility of profound romantic connection. On the other hand, if I practice exercising compassionate empathy for myself, I'll begin welcoming myself wholly into my life, allowing me to accept both myself and the real world around me. Of course, this includes everyone I encounter—even that promising prospect of romantic love. Though this may seem unlikely, even scary at first, the first steps toward meeting the challenge to own my life and welcome others into it quickly change into an irresistible adventure that will completely alter the complexion of the everyday.

One of the most unexpected lessons of this adventure is the realization that, when I "get it wrong" and mess things up, acceptance of myself and connection with others is necessary to "getting it right" and straightening things out again. Otherwise, without a loving connection with myself, I won't even be able to identify the parts of myself about which I have to be able to tell the truth so that reconciliation and healing can take place.

In his evaluation of our culture's relationship with psychiatry and psychiatric medication, Charles Barber (2008) remarks, "In perhaps the most ironic development in the neuro-revolution, psychotherapy, and, indeed, social experience (have) been shown to change the brain at a structural and functional level in ways that can be comparable to drugs."[1]

That experience changes us is a truism. Learning modifies connections among neurons, thus changing neural network activity. Profound empathetic experience—intimacy with myself and others—is a robust and profoundly effective treatment that reaches even the biological level. At the same time, research shows that empathy without compassion increases negative feelings, while empathy followed by compassion training increases positive emotions (Klimecki et al. 2013). Compassion, then, is necessary for circumventing empathic failure, burnout, defensive detachment, and aggression toward self and others.

The same processes apply to learning about the gaps between the crazy story I've long told myself about me, the real story behind my crazy, the stories I tell myself about the world around me, and the world's real story. Relationship sanity makes room for processing all of these and then creating a reality-based story (or stories) about myself and the world, none of which need to make me feel that I must resort to throwing blame at everyone and everything and then running away.

Finding my way into love is a revolution against the occupying force of irrelationship. Paradoxically, this revolution requires not defeating, but *connecting with* the pain, fear, and loneliness that have long driven my crazy. Choosing to make these connections and walk the road of relationship sanity is to reclaim my birthright to give and to receive love, and to be transformed by both.

ACKNOWLEDGMENTS

From Mark Borg

This book is dedicated to you, Haruna Miyamoto-Borg because you challenge me every day be a loving, generous, and kind version of myself. It is true what Isa (the woman who married us) said, "You can fall in love every day."

Kata and Uta, being your father—your *otosan*—and loving you is joy beyond measure.

Eve Golden has been my beloved ally, source of strength, and long-time psychoanalytic editor *par excellence* from the very start of this process of taking experience and thought and putting it in flight.

As always, Gareth Esersky, my/our agent, has provided the consistent guidance and care for my work, and that of the Irrelationship Group, that undergirds this volume. Thank you, Gareth, for taking me, and for taking Danny, Grant and I, on. Being represented by you makes me feel like the luckiest dude on earth. Working with you and the Carol Mann Agency is among the greatest gifts of this whole writing sojourn.

Central Recovery Press, especially Patrick Hughes, Valerie Killeen, and Kelly Elcock, thank you! Authorship with CRP has been, as was offered when we began back in 2014, a synergistic partnership. I feel empowered by the love, care, and support that I received from you as a member of the Irrelationship Project, and throughout the development of this solo endeavor.

Joanna Murphy, thank you for your guidance and care—for walking with me on this road and shining consistently a loving light of spirit.

The raucous band, All Nite Rave, was my earliest attempt to form and maintain a collaboration that was challenged to survive the clashing of egos of its many parents. Through dozens of members, it wound up being the cherished, idealized lovechild of Jim DeLozier (RIP) and I. We alone survived *it*—the original name of what Freud called "das *Id*," that raging, instinctual component of the unconscious mind that's ever at war with the ego, whose job it is to navigate consensus reality. I love you, Jim, as there is no one who sailed with me more consistently and closely toward treacherous shores. Oh, how I miss you.

Chris Borg—we live, Bro (big Styrofoam rafts drifting out to sea notwithstanding)! I love you, and am so grateful to have you in my life.

Seal Beach Surf Crew (a.k.a. Midnight Surf Team): Greg Hex, Mike Dalla, John Turi, Bill Zunkel. Soul mates, all. God, how I love you!

Kristy Matthews, who would I be without you? All these years; all this love and magic. Thank you.

Terry and Joan DeLozier. The world is not the same without Jim and I'm disoriented in ways I continue to discover. The love and refuge you gave us Corona del Mar punks still lives inside me.

My marriage notwithstanding, my relationships with Dr. Grant Brenner and Danny Berry via the Irrelationship Project represent the most contemporary shape my aspiration toward collaboration has taken. While we're not all comfortable with me comparing this project to a marriage, I can say it remains among my most rewarding experiences. Project #3: Thanks guys.

Matt Stedman, much gratitude for the calming, nurturing counsel on our surf sojourns up and down the East Coast. Cowabunga, dude!

Also, thank you, Dr. Jeanne Henry for taking me under your wing at Newport Harbor Adolescent Psychiatric Hospital, showing me the ropes, and opening the door to the vast, amazing field of mental health care. Thank you, Dr. Ronda Hampton, my professional soul mate, for the years of shoulder-to-shoulder camaraderie on the front lines of community crisis intervention in Avalon Gardens, South Central Los Angeles. Dr. Maggie Decker, I'm so grateful for your guidance, care, love, and supervision at AIDS Service Foundation in the mid-1990s. These three experiences have formed the central core of my professional identity and I carry you with me every day through what often feels like *clinical mayhem*. I love this work, and you three have made that possible.

PR *par excellence*, Kelli Daniel of Dart Frogg—you rock!

Thank you, Charlotte Rolland for giving me a consistent love that proved itself in action. I believe all these years since you've been gone sets the cornerstone of my willingness and ability to love and be loved.

Thank you, Charlotte and Jon Rysanek. Fixing what was broken between us has been among the most miraculous examples of what love can do. I'm so grateful for the love we share, and so happy for the love shared between my beloved Grrrrrrrrls—Haruna, Kata, and Uta—and their Nana and Papa.

Thank you, Sandy Borg for an excellent evening of lion-taming. Its benefits express themselves in my life every day, thirty-one years, and counting, later. And thanks Erik Borg for *also* loving me through all that—and this.

Love and gratitude to you, Mark Borg and Bonnie Mankoff. Your steady thoughtfulness and kindness maintain our connection across miles and years.

I'm deeply grateful for Osamu and Yoko Miyamoto. I love you, and I believe I hit the jackpot in the in-law department. *Arigato gozaimasu* for all the love and generosity you consistently shower upon your NYC family no matter the geographic distance.

Wil Diaz, what in the world would I do without our early morning walks in the East Village?! Much, much love, man!

Cheers to the snarling wolverines in the back row, especially you, Ronnie Sawyer and Mary Jane Rambo!

Special mention (again) to those mods and punks, surfers, shrinks, black sheep, iconoclasts, colleagues, mentors, supervisors, and soul mates who, from a vast array of time periods and contexts, have loved and were loved by me in ways that still fuel a wider and ever-expanding *raison d'être*. Special thanks to: Bill Defina, Britt Huycke, Karin Nance, Phil Vock, Megan Hardy, Byron Abel, Robert Taube, Glenn Parish, Paul Loringer, Steve Torrey, Scott Murdock, Cheo Rodriguez, Liz Rusch, Eric Lee, Marty Strom, Emily Garrod, Mik Manenti, Stuart Pyle, Marcus Ho, Susan Greenfield, Tom Cox, Emily Damron-Cox, Paco and Maiken Lozano-Wiese, Rob Gutfliesh, Helmut Krackie, Scott Graham, James Kwon, Pat Kenary, Bobbi Fuentes, Rie Ogura, James Gary, Sr., Machiko Makabe, David Kopstein, Scott Stewart, Jonathan Schnappe, Kumi Hirose, Tim Barnes, Mark Lanaghan, Molly Goldman, Dave Jawor, Gloria Robotham, Elizabeth Shanahan, Isa Stanfels, John Henry Eldridge, Norman Karns, Shawn Marie Turi, John Hatchett, Daniel Leyva, Father Michael Lynch, Maureen Kamsi-Storey, Joerg Bose, Sandra Buechler, Jack Drescher, Sue Kolod, Brent Willock, Jack Eppler, Kako Takeuchi, Zeke and Sheila Zimmerman, John Flikeid, Connie Rolland, Jules Cohen, Hara Estroff-Marano, John Ellert, Scott Munsey, Jennifer McCarroll, Chana Pollack, Myra Mniewski, Matt Dalton, Elise Cox, Stuart Lachs, Mike Moore, Barry Williams, Ken Robidoux, Mauri Helffrich, David Lester, Gary Ireland, John Lance Harrison, Amy Kerr, Tim Couch, Sean Carver, Wendy and Kim Marshall, Paul Tully, Daniel MacNamee, and Brendan Rafferty. The combined force of your love, all of you, is what gives me the will to traverse through—and sustains my every step into—whatever it is that comes next, and then after that.

From Grant Brenner

There are so many people to acknowledge in the making of this book, and I can only mention a few, and am sure to forget many. First, my co-authors Mark and Danny, for bringing "self-irrelationship" to fruition. My family has been supportive in allowing me the time to work on this project. Our publisher CRP, especially Valerie Killeen and all their wonderful and supportive staff, as well as our agent Gareth Esersky at Carol Mann Agency and Pam Liflander for advising us early on with this book. I am grateful to the psychoanalytic institute where I trained in individual psychoanalysis and organizational psychodynamics; the William Alanson White Institute and the many teachers and mentors there; various teachers in study groups, notably Lewis Aron who taught us so much about relational analysis and how to deeply think through complex material, Mark Blechner for cultivating a profound and living appreciation for dreams and group process, and Jay Greenberg for conveying an understanding the many different Sigmund Freuds one can interpret in his many works, along with the myriad clinicians and researchers upon whose work we have drawn. I would like to acknowledge the people who have sought help from me over the years, from whom I have learned, and for the common good in humanity as we slowly overcome stigma and embrace well-being.

NOTES

Introduction

1 Bateson, Gregory. *Steps to an Ecology of Mind: Collected Essays in Anthropology, Psychiatry, Evolution, and Epistemology.* Chicago, 1-3.

2 Bateson, Gregory, Don D. Jackson, Jay Haley, and John Weakland. "Toward a Theory of Schizophrenia," 251-264.

3 James, William. Goodreads, Webpage title: William James > Quotes > Quotable Quote, Date on website of first "like": Jan 31, 2009, Website description: "the world's largest site for readers and book recommendations". (Accessed goodreads.com on January 14, 2019)

4 Khan, Masud, "The Concept of Cumulative Trauma," 306.

5 Stephen Porges's Polyvagal Theory explained why knowing that we are seen and heard by important people in our lives can make us feel calm and safe, and why being ignored or dismissed can lead to rage and mental collapse. We are highly attuned to subtle emotional shifts in other people. Our mirror neurons register their inner experience, and our bodies make internal adjustments accordingly. This theory supports the notion that our brains are built to help us function in community—and that most of our energy is devoted to connecting to others (Porges 2011).

6 Karlen Lyons-Ruth and Deborah Block (1996) found that emotional distance and role-reversal (in which mothers expected their children to look after them) are specifically related to aggressive behaviors toward self and others starting in young adulthood.

7 A psychoanalytic term for acting out unconscious feelings relationally—that is, co-acting out, or playing out, our feelings in interaction rather than consciously experiencing or being aware of them. In relational psychoanalysis the term *enactment* is used to describe the non-reflecting playing out of a mental scenario, rather than verbally describing the associated thoughts and feelings. The term *enactment* was first introduced by Theodore Jacobs (1986)

to describe the re-actualization of unsymbolized and unconscious emotional experiences involved in the relationship between the patient and the therapist. More precisely, Jacobs refers to the countertransference enactment, thus highlighting the implications of the personality characteristics, affective frame, representations, and analyst's conflicts for the patient and the interactional behavior. Currently, the concept of enactment is usually used to explain the re-experience of a role assumed during childhood, which is recited on the stage of the therapist's consulting room: the analyst is given a specific role to play; in this context, both the patient and the analyst lose their sense of distance, interacting with each other verbally and nonverbally, leading to intra-psychic dynamics in the form of interactions within the therapeutic setting (Aron 1996). In the perspective of relational psychoanalysis, the central aspect of therapeutic change is given by the liberation of the patient and the analyst from the repetitive unconscious patterns due to the reflective awareness' acquisition of the relational interchange and the contribution of both parties. Traumatized patients, especially, tend to bond with their therapists not so much through words as through enactments, expressing unconsciously—by the action—the dissociated aspects of the self and the object representation (Bromberg 1998, 2011).

8 The pioneering French psychologist and philosopher Pierre Janet was the first to show clearly and systematically how it is the most direct psychological defense against overwhelming traumatic experiences. He demonstrated that dissociative phenomena play an important role in widely divergent post-traumatic stress responses, which he included under the nineteenth-century diagnosis of hysteria. His dissociation theory is based on nine concepts developed or elaborated by Janet: psychological automatism, consciousness, subconsciousness, narrowed field of consciousness, dissociation, amnesia, suggestibility, fixed idea, and emotion.

9 A condition of great fascination and much misunderstanding in popular culture (unfortunately, for those who live with it), dissociative identity disorder (DID) is thought to a significant degree to be the result of severe early trauma. Contributing factors include emotional, physical, and sexual abuse, as well as neglect and chronic gaslighting by caregivers who are unable to provide a basic developmental environment. These factors, when combined with a proclivity for dissociation, can lead to a profound disruption of sense of self, resulting in the aforementioned "multiple personalities." The catch is that those with DID do not actually have many different personalities. Instead, they have subsystems of personality that are not integrated with one another. These subsystems represent different aspects of the more coherent and cohesive personality that would exist in the presence of a more healthy developmental experience. The different subsystems tend to form pairs and subgroups which represent different aspects of and responses to trauma.

Some people appear to be more prone to dissociation than others, with a greater facility for fluidity of identity, often a highly adaptive social trait. In the absence of trauma, such folk may be more capable of taking on multiple perspectives, seeing things from many different angles, an inherently healthy way to be in the world characterized by less conflict when different perspectives are in communication and can coexist well. They may be able to move from role to role, or occupy a role so completely as to seem like the original, even hyper-authentic and more original than the original itself. Think about actors who can seem to become another person as part of their craft, or politicians who are able to wear many faces with ease. To an extent, the ability to pivot, to take on the right persona for the right situation, is very adaptive. But when it leads to hiding things from oneself, we end up tripping ourselves up, leading to scandals, grievous errors in judgment, and bad decisions we don't even know why we made.

10 Making a strong point, Janina Fisher (2017) says that while splitting is an ingenious and adaptive survival strategy, the price for living with parts of self split off is high: "Aware that their self-presentation and ability to function is only one piece of who they really are, they now feel fraudulent" (19). Later, Fisher also asserts, "dissociative splitting is a mental ability, not just a symptom" (245). Because dissociation is considered developmentally to be one of the earliest defenses human beings use, we tie dissociation in with human nature, one of the basic frameworks required for maintaining a sense of personal identity and shared social reality. Psychologically, we distort understanding, self-perception, social impressions, and so on, in order to keep things moving along. Sometimes this is done through inadvertent, unconscious bias, while at other times it is enacted through motivated self-deception and willful misdirection of others.

11 Sullivan's theory of dissociation and *not-me* experience is summarized by Feist and Feist (2008, 222–23) as follows: "During mid-infancy a child acquires three me personifications (bad-me, good-me, and not-me) that form the building blocks of the self personification. Each is related to the evolving conception of me or my body. The *bad-me personification* is fashioned from experiences of punishment and disapproval that infants receive from their mothering one. The resulting anxiety is strong enough to teach infants that they are bad, but it is not so severe as to cause the experience to be dissociated or *selectively inattended*. Like all personifications, the bad-me is shaped out of the interpersonal situation; that is, infants can learn that they are bad only from someone else, ordinarily the bad-mother. The *good-me personification* results from infants' experiences with reward and approval. Infants feel good about themselves when they perceive their mother's expressions of tenderness. Such experiences diminish anxiety and foster the good-me personification. Sudden severe anxiety, however, may cause an infant to

form the *not-me personification* and to dissociate experiences related to that anxiety."

Chapter One: How Self-Irrelationship Looks and Feels

1 Paraphrased from Freud, Sigmund. "Remembering, Repeating and Working Though."

2 The realm of co-created psychological defense that we eventually termed "irrelationship" was born in a chapter written by Mark in *The Psychology of Expectations*, published in 2010, entitled "Human Antidepressants and the Old Song-and-Dance Routine: Zeroing in on the Life-Course (and Lack Thereof) of Expectations in Clinical Practice." "Human antidepressant" as then framed wasn't *self-irrelationship*. But it analyzed compulsive caretaking as a defense against the anxieties associated with intimacy.

3 The safety provided by sensitive attunement between parent and infant facilitates the child's experience and expression of emotion, obviating the need for avoidant strategies. For the child, safety includes not being left alone with negative emotional states. Otherwise, the child will have difficulty learning to manage emotional difficulties later in life, leading to difficulty in relationships. Good caretaking includes a corrective experience of *interactive repair* (Tronick 1989, 2007).

4 Janina Fisher (2017, 61) says that "(a)lthough human beings tend to put words to experiences of empathy ("I feel understood—it feels like someone 'gets it'—I feel like you believe me"), attunement and empathy are actually nonverbal, somatic experiences of warmth, relaxation, being able to breathe more deeply, and feeling emotionally closer and more connected."

5 According to the *Diagnostic and Statistical Manual of Mental Disorders* (DSM-5)—the psychiatric diagnostic manual published by the American Psychiatric Association—in order to meet criteria for dissociative identity disorder, a person must exhibit at least two distinct personality states. Each personality state must have its own "relatively enduring pattern of perceiving, relating to and thinking about the environment and the self." Furthermore, the personality states must be cut off from one another, involving "marked discontinuity in sense of self and sense of agency," with symptoms in other areas involving thinking, emotion, and behavior. Notably, those with DID may experience a sense of "possession," as in having one's mind and body taken over by a malevolent spirit. Another hallmark of DID is loss of memory of important events and actions, traumatic events, and even ordinary, nontraumatic events. Memory is therefore "state-dependent." What happens in one emotional state or context may not be recalled in another. The remaining DSM-5 criteria for DID are common to all psychiatric disorders: the symptoms cause significant distress and/or dysfunction that

can't be accounted for by another condition, such as another psychiatric disorder, a substance use disorder, or a medical disorder; or, in rare cases, by malingering or factitious disorder. Before diagnosis, many with DID are diagnosed with other conditions such as depression, anxiety, substance abuse, or personality disorders. Those with DID are often unaware of shifts in their personality state. For example, they may abruptly move from a state of accommodation and kindness to one of hostility and mistrust with no consciousness of the change, while those around them may be startled by it. When confronted, they may accuse their "accuser" of thinking them incompetent—a readily available means of deflecting attention from their own behavior. They also may unwittingly find themselves in company with people who know more about them than they know about themselves, having unknowingly communicated information about themselves when in a dissociated state.

6 Searles, *Countertransference*, 380.

7 Glen (a pseudonym) is Mark's patient. The first-person narration comes from Mark's clinical case notes. They are used with Glen's permission.

8 Van der Kolk reports that, according to Charles Darwin, mammalian emotions are fundamentally rooted in biology, and are the indispensable source of motivation to initiate action, giving shape and direction to whatever we do. Their primary expression is through the muscles of the face and body, which communicate our mental state and intention to others. The fundamental purpose of emotions is to initiate movement that will restore the organism to safety and physical equilibrium (75).

9 Searles, *Countertransference*, 380.

10 Bowlby, "The Nature of the Child's Tie to His Mother," 354.

11 In fact, neuropsychologist Allen Schore (2001) says that the cornerstone of infant attachment is what he calls "adaptive projective identification." Fisher (2017, 258) describes this process as follows: it is the way in which an infant's distress, projected via dysregulation, is experienced by parents as their own distress. The baby cries; the parent is dysregulated by the cries. She feels uncomfortable, so much so that she is driven to pick the baby up, soothe, comfort, and distract, until the repair effort hits on the infant's unmet need and the baby calms and settles into the parent's arms. Only then does the parent's nervous system calm and settle. All is well now—both are regulated and soothed."

12 Fromm, *The Art of Loving*, 18–19.

13 James, William. Goodreads, Webpage title: William James > Quotes > Quotable Quote, Date on website of first "like": Jan 31, 2009, Website description: "the world's largest site for readers and book recommendations". (Accessed goodreads.com on January 14, 2019)

Chapter Four: The GRAFTS Behaviors: How Childhood Experiences Keep Us Crazy

1 Bromberg, "Standing in the Spaces: The Multiplicity of Self and the Psychoanalytic Relationship," 509–539.

2 Siegel, *The Developing Mind*, 26.

Chapter Seven: A Good Enough World: From Self-Irrelationship to Better Relationships

1 This pattern was described by Sigmund Freud in his 1920 essay "Beyond the Pleasure Principle." He observed a child throwing his favorite toy from his crib, becoming upset at the loss, then reeling the toy back in, only to replay this action repetitively. Such behavior is often observed in children when they throw a toy out of reach, then cry for it to be retrieved. Freud theorized that children are attempting to master the sensation of loss, possibly using the toy as a surrogate for their mothers, who cannot always be physically present.

Freud believed there are two ways the past is relived: 1) through memories, or 2) through actions, such as in repetition compulsion. Schools of thought vary on how they view the concept of repetition; for example, the passive type, in which a person consistently chooses familiar experiences as a means of dealing with problems from the past, such as staying in a situation of pain and chaos instead of risking traumatic new experiences. Another might balk at new experiences for fear that they will be more painful than their present situation.

Another school of thought suggests a participatory form of repetition in which a person actively engages in behavior that mimics an earlier stressor, either deliberately or unconsciously. In such cases, terrifying childhood experiences may become sources of attraction in adulthood. For instance, a person who was spanked as a child may incorporate this into their adult sexual practices, or a victim of sexual abuse may attempt to seduce a person in authority in their life, such as a boss or therapist. Psychoanalysts describe this as an attempt at *mastery* of their feelings and experience, in the sense that they unconsciously want to go through the same situation, but with a different outcome than was experienced in the past. This view is based on the notion that behavior may be due to "psychodynamic factors," driven by motivations and emotional states we are not aware of.

Trauma theories provide complements and alternatives to the unconscious motivation model, however. This may be a form of fundamental attribution error therapists ironically use with patients, "blaming the victim" by postulating a "need" to engage in self-harm. Sometimes these behaviors are driven by masochism and mastery, but they are often the result of early traumatic conditioning, protective mechanisms wired in during childhood that persist into adulthood without any primary meaning or intent. Distinguishing habit from motivated behavior is critical, as well as understanding the relationships between the two in adult life.

Chapter Nine: Self-Self Assessment: The 40-20-40
1 Interestingly, many years after we initially began publishing our work on the 40-20-40—stating a dynamic of reciprocity where people are encouraged to contribute *no less than 40 percent and no more than 60 percent* to their relationships—Neuropsychologist and psychoanalyst Mark Solms (2021) discusses a dynamic state of reciprocity that he calls the 60:40 rule. He states that "The 60:40 rule is an innate social rule. It demands reciprocity and mutuality, and therefore facilitates the development of empathy—that is, the capacity to read other minds" (234).

Chapter Ten: Making Your Crazy Work for You: The DREAM Sequence
1 "The theory of structural dissociation of the personality proposes that patients with complex trauma-related disorders are characterized by a division of their personality into different prototypical parts, each with its own psychobiological underpinnings. As one or more apparently normal parts (ANPs), patients have a propensity toward engaging in evolutionary prepared action systems for adaptation to daily living to guide their actions. Two or more emotional parts (EPs) are fixated in traumatic experience. As EPs, patients predominantly engage action systems related to physical defense and attachment cry. ANP and EP are insufficiently integrated, but interact and share a number of dispositions of the personality (e.g., speaking). All parts are stuck in maladaptive action tendencies that maintain dissociation, including a range of phobias, which is a major focus of this article. Phase-oriented treatment helps patients gradually develop adaptive mental and behavioral actions, thus overcoming their phobias and structural dissociation. Phase 1, symptom reduction and stabilization, is geared toward overcoming phobias of mental contents, dissociative parts, and attachment and attachment loss with the therapist. Phase 2, treatment of traumatic memories, is directed toward overcoming the phobia of traumatic memories, and phobias related to insecure attachment to the perpetrator(s), particularly in EPs. In Phase 3, integration and rehabilitation, treatment is focused on overcoming phobias of normal life, healthy risk-taking and change, and intimacy." (Steele, van der Hart, Onno & Ellert, 2005). https://pubmed.ncbi.nlm.nih.gov/16172081/

Chapter Twelve: Repair

1 The social psychologist Erich Fromm (1941, 101) believed that "all are in need of help and depend on one another. Human solidarity is the necessary condition for the unfolding of any one individual." This is a guiding principle for understanding interactive repair, and a reminder of why we must continue to grapple with the pain and uncertainty of working through irrelationship—to find each other, to find ourselves.

Chapter Fifteen: Mutuality with Myself

1 Psychological resilience is defined as an individual's ability to properly adapt to stress and adversity (American Psychological Association 2010). Stress and adversity can come in the shape of family or relationship problems, health problems, or workplace and financial stressors, among others. Individuals demonstrate resilience when they can face difficult experiences and rise above them with ease. Resilience is not a rare ability; in reality, it is found in the average individual and it can be learned and developed by virtually anyone (Southwick, Litz, Charney, and Friedman 2011). Resilience should be considered a process rather than a trait. A common misconception about resilient people is that they experience no negative emotions or thoughts and display optimism in all situations. In reality, however, resiliency is demonstrated in individuals who can effectively navigate their way around crises and use effective methods of coping. In other words, people who demonstrate resilience are people with positive emotionality; they effectively balance negative emotions with positive ones (Southwick and Charney 2012). According to Steven Southwick and Dennis Charney, resilience is composed of particular factors attributed to an individual. Numerous factors cumulatively contribute to a person's resilience, the primary one being positive relationships inside or outside one's family. It is the single most critical means of handling both ordinary and extraordinary levels of stress. These positive relationships include traits such as mutual, reciprocal support and caring. Such relationships bolster a person's resilience. Studies also identify other factors that develop and sustain resilience:

- The ability to make realistic plans and to follow through with them.
- A positive self-concept and confidence in one's strengths and abilities.
- Communication and problem-solving skills.
- The ability to manage strong impulses and feelings.

Conclusion: Letting Your Crazy Work for You

1 Charles Barber, *Comfortably Numb*, 191.

BIBLIOGRAPHY

Acevedo, Bianca P., Arthur Aron, Helen E. Fisher, and Lucy L. Brown. "Neural Correlates of Long-Term Intense Romantic Love." *Social Cognitive & Affective Neuroscience* 7, no. 2 (2011): 145–159.

Ainsworth, Mary D. S. "The Development of Infant-Mother Attachment." In *Review of Child Development Research, Child Development and Social Policy Volume 3,* edited by Bettye Cardwell and Henry N. Ricciuti, 1-94. Chicago: University of Chicago Press, 1973.

American Psychiatric Association. *Diagnostic and Statistical Manual of Mental Disorders,* 5th ed. Arlington, VA: APA, 2013.

American Psychological Association. "The Road to Resilience." Retrieved June 14, 2010, from http://www.appleseeds.org/10-Ways-Build-Resilience_APA.htm, 2014.

Aron, Lew. *A Meeting of the Minds: Mutuality in Psychoanalysis.* Hillsdale, NJ: The Analytic Press, 1996.

Barber, Charles. *Comfortably Numb: How Psychiatry Is Medicating a Nation.* New York: Vintage Books, 2008.

Bateson, Gregory. *Steps to an Ecology of Mind: Collected Essays in Anthropology, Psychiatry, Evolution, and Epistemology.* Chicago: University Of Chicago Press, 1972.

Bateson, Gregory, Don D. Jackson, Jay Haley, and John Weakland. "Toward a Theory of Schizophrenia." *Behavioral Science,* vol. 1 (1956): 251–264.

Beyarslan, Sila D., Uzer, Tugba. "Psychological Control and Indulgent Parenting Predict Emotional-Abuse Victimization in Romantic Relationships." *Current Psychology,* (2020): 10.1007/s12144-020-01072-w.

Bion, Wilfred R. "The Psycho-Analytical Study of Thinking." *International Journal of Psycho-Analysis*, v. 43 (1962): 306-310.

Borg, Jr., M. B. "Psychoanalytic Pure War: Interactions with the Post-Apocalyptic Unconscious." *Journal for the Psychoanalysis of Culture and Society*, 8, no. 1 (2003): 57-67.

Borg, Jr., Mark B. "Community Group-Analysis: A Post-Crisis Synthesis." *Group-Analysis* 36, no. 2 (2003): 228-241.

Borg, Jr., Mark B. "Human Antidepressants and the Old Song-and-Dance Routine: Zeroing in on the Life-Course (and Lack Thereof) of Expectations in Clinical Practice." In P. León and N. Tamez (Eds.) *The Psychology of Expectations*, 165-169. Happague, NY: Nova Science Publishers, 2010.

Borg, Jr., Mark B., Grant H. Brenner, and John Daniel Berry. *Irrelationship: How We Use Dysfunctional Relationships to Hide from Intimacy.* Las Vegas, NV: Central Recovery Press, 2015.

Borg, Jr., Mark B., Grant H. Brenner, and John Daniel Berry. "The Disposable Person—Being Unvalued in the Modern Age." *Psychology Today* (August 27, 2015). https://tinyurl.com/yagav7w9

Borg, Jr., Mark B., Grant H. Brenner, and John Daniel Berry. "Passion Precluded: Irrelationship and the Cost of Co-Created Psychological Defenses." In *Psychoanalytic Perspectives on Passion: Meanings and Manifestations in the Clinical Setting and Beyond,* 135-144). Edited by Brent Willock, Rebecca Curtis, and Lori Bohm. London: Routledge, 2017.

Borg, Jr., Mark B., Grant H. Brenner, and John Daniel Berry. *Relationship Sanity: Creating and Maintaining Healthy Relationships.* Las Vegas, NV: Central Recovery Press, 2018.

Bornstein, Marc H., Arterberry, Martha E., Mash, Clay, and Manian, Nanmathi. "Discrimination of Facial Expression by 5-Month-Old Infants of Nondepressed and Clinically Depressed Mothers." *Infant Behavior and Development* 34, no. 1 (2011): 100-106. https://doi.org/10.1016/j.infbeh.2010.10.002.

Bornstein, Robert. "Depathologizing Dependency." *The Journal of Nervous and Mental Disease* 186, no. 2 (February 1998): 67-73.

Bose, Joerg. "Trauma, Depression, and Mourning." *Contemporary Psychoanalysis* 31, no. 3 (1995): 399–407.

Bose, Joerg. "The Inhumanity of the Other: Treating Trauma and Depression." *The Review of Interpersonal Psychoanalysis* 3, no. 1 (1998): 1–4.

Boston Change Process Study Group. "Engagement and the Emergence of a Charged Other." *Contemporary Psychoanalysis* 54, no. 2 (2019): 540–559.

Bowlby, John. "The Nature of the Child's Tie to His Mother." *International Journal of Psychoanalysis* 39 (1958): 350–371.

Bowlby John. *Attachment and Loss Volume 1: Attachment.* New York: Basic Books, 1969.

Bromberg, Philip, M. "Standing in the Spaces: The Multiplicity of Self and the Psychoanalytic Relationship." *Contemporary Psychoanalysis* 32 (1996): 509–539.

Bromberg, Philip, M. *Standing in the Spaces: Essays on Clinical Process, Trauma, and Dissociation.* New York: Routledge, 1998.

Bromberg, Philip, M. *The Shadow of the Tsunami: and the Growth of the Relational Mind.* New York: Routledge Taylor & Francis Group, 2011.

Buechler, Sandra. *Psychoanalytic Approaches to Problems in Living: Addressing Life's Challenges in Clinical Practice.* London: Routledge, 2019.

Carli, Linda, L. "Cognitive Reconstruction, Hindsight, and Reactions to Victims and Perpetrators." *Society for Personality and Social Psychology* 25, no. 8 (1999): 966–979.

Carnes, Patrick, Debra Laaser, and Mark Laaser. *Open Hearts: Renewing Relationships with Recovery, Romance, and Reality.* Wickenburg, AZ: Gentle Path Press, 1999.

Carter, C. Sue. "Oxytocin Pathways and the Evolution of Human Behavior." Annual Review of Psychology 65 (2014): 17–39.

Christiansen, Linda. "Finding Voice: Learning about Language and Power." *Voices from the Middle* 18, no. 3 (2011): 9–17.

Dias, Brian G. and Kerry J. Ressler. "Parental Olfactory Experience Influences Behavior and Neural Structure in Subsequent Generations." *Natural Neuroscience* 17, 89–96 (2014). https://doi.org/10.1038/nn.3594

Eley, Thalia C., Tom A. McAdams, Fruhling V. Rijsdijk, Paul Lichtenstein, Jurgita Narusyte, David Reiss, Erica L. Spotts, Jody M. Ganiban, and Jenae M. Neiderhiser. "The Intergenerational Transmission of Anxiety: A Children-of-Twins Study." *American Journal of Psychiatry*, April 23, 2015. appi.ajp.2015.14070818. doi:10.1176/appi.ajp.2015.14070818.

Feist, Jess, and Gregory J. Feist. *Theories of Personality, 7th Edition.* New York: McGraw-Hill, 2008.

Fisher, Janina. *Healing the Fragmented Selves of Trauma Survivors: Overcoming Internal Self-Alienation.* New York: Routledge, 2017.

Freud, Sigmund. "Remembering, Repeating and Working Though." In *Standard Edition of the Complete Works of Sigmund Freud, Vol. 12,* 145–156. London: The Hogarth Press, 1914.

Freud, Sigmund. "Mourning and Melancholia." In *Standard Edition of the Complete Works of Sigmund Freud, Vol. 14,* 237–258. London: The Hogarth Press, 1917.

Freud, Sigmund. "Beyond the Pleasure Principle." In *Standard Edition of the Complete Works of Sigmund Freud, Vol. 18,* 3–64. London: The Hogarth Press, 1920.

Freyd, Jennifer J. "Betrayal trauma." In *Encyclopedia of Psychological Trauma,* 76. Edited by G. Reyes, J.D. Elhai, & J.D.Ford (Eds). New York: John Wiley & Sons, 2008.

Fromm, Erich. *The Art of Loving.* New York: Harper & Row, 1956.

Gobin, R.L. and J.J. Freyd. "Betrayal and Revictimization: Preliminary Findings." *Psychological Trauma: Theory, Research, Practice, and Policy,* 1 (2009): 242-257

Goldklank, Shelly. "The Shoop Shoop Song: A Guide to Psychoanalytic-Systemic Couple Therapy." *Contemporary Psychoanalysis* 45 no. 1 (2009): 3-25.

Harris, Michelle A., and Orth, Ulrich. "The Link Between Self-Esteem and Social Relationships: A Meta-Analysis of Longitudinal Studies." *Journal of Personality and Social*

Psychology (2019). http://dx.doi.org/10.1037/pspp0000265

Hendrix, Harville. *Getting the Love You Want: A Guide for Couples.* New York: Henry Holt and Company, 2008.

Herman, Judith L. *Trauma and Recovery: The Aftermath of Violence—From Domestic Abuse to Political Terror.* New York: Basic Books, 1992.

Howell, Elizabeth F. & Itzkowitz, Sheldon, eds. *The Dissociative Mind in Psychoanalysis: Understanding and Working with Trauma.* New York, NY: Routledge, 2013.

Iacoviello, Brian M., Dennis S. Charney. "Psychosocial Facets of Resilience: Implications for Preventing Post-trauma Psychopathology, Treating Trauma Survivors, and Enhancing Community Resilience." *European Journal of Psychotraumatology* (October, 2014): 1–5.

Insel, Thomas R. "The Challenge of Translation in Social Neuroscience: A Review of Oxytocin, Vasopressin, and Affiliative Behavior." Neuron 65, no. 6 (2010): 768–779.

Jacobs, Theodor. "On Countertransference Enactments." *Journal of the American Psychoanalytic Association,* 34 (1986): 289–307.

James, William. Goodreads, Webpage title: William James > Quotes > Quotable Quote, Date on website of first "like": Jan 31, 2009, Website description: "the world's largest site for readers and book recommendations". (Accessed goodreads.com on January 14, 2019)

Johnson, Susan. Love Sense: The Revolutionary New Science of Romantic Relationships. New York: Little, Brown and Company, 2013.

Keats, John. The Complete Poetical Works and Letters of John Keats, 277. Cambridge, MA: Houghton, Mifflin and Company, 1899.

Khan, Masud. "The Concept of Cumulative Trauma." *Psychoanalytic Study of the Child* 18, no 1 (1963): 286-306.

Klimecki, Olga M., Susan Leilberg,, Claus Lamm, and Tania Singer. "Functional Neural Plasticity and Associated Changes in Positive Affect after Compassion Training." *Cerebral Cortex* 23, no. 7 (2013): 1552–1561.

Lerner, Melvin, J. "The Justice Motive: Some Hypotheses as to Its Origins and Forms." *Journal of Personality* 45, no. 1 (1977): 1-52.

Lerner, Melvin J. and Carolyn H. Simmons. "Observer's Reaction to the 'Innocent Victim': Compassion or Rejection?" *Journal of Personality and Social Psychology* 4, no. 2 (1966): 203-210.

Love, Tiffany M. "Oxytocin, Motivation and the Role of Dopamine." Pharmacology, Biochemistry and Behavior 119 (2014): 49-60.

Lovelace, Linda and McGrady, Mike. *Ordeal.* Secaucus, New Jersey: Citadel, 1980.

Lyons-Ruth, Karlen and Deborah Block. "The Disturbed Caregiving System: Relations among Childhood Trauma, Maternal Caregiving, and Infant Affect and Attachment." *Infant Mental Health Journal* 17, no. 3 (1996): 257-275.

Metz, Michael. "Exploring the Complexity of High School Students' Beliefs about Language Variation." Linguistics and Education 45, no. 1 (2018): 10-19.

Porges, Stephen S. *The Polyvagal Theory: Neurophysiological Foundations of Emotions, Communication and Self-Regulation.* New York: W. W. Norton & Company, 2011.

Reich, Wilhelm. *Character Analysis.* New York: Farrar, Straus and Giroux, 1933 (1980).

Ross, Lee. "The Intuitive Psychologist and His Shortcomings: Distortions in the Attribution Process." *Advances in Experimental Social Psychology* 10, no. 1 (1977): 173-220.

Schore, Allen N. "Neurobiology, Developmental Psychology, and Psychoanalysis: Convergent Findings on the Subject of Projective Identification." In *Being Alive: Building on the Work of Anne Alvarez,* 57-76. Edited by Judith Edwards, New York: Brunner-Routledge, 2001.

Searles, Harold. *Countertransference.* New York: Jason Aronson, 1979.

Sette, Giovanna, Gabrielle Coppola, and Rosalina Cassibba. "The Transmission of Attachment across Generations: The State of Art and New Theoretical Perspectives." Scandinavian Journal of Psychology 56, no. 3 (2015): 315-26.

Shaw, Daniel. *Traumatic Narcissism: Relational Systems of Subjugation.* New York: Routledge, 2014.

Siegel, Dan J. *The Developing Mind: Toward a Neurobiology of Interpersonal Experience.* New York: Guilford Press, 1999.

Solms, Mark. *The Hidden Spring: A Journey to the Source of Consciousness.* New York: W. W. Norton & Company, 2021.

Southwick, Steven M., and Dennis S. Charney. *Resilience: The Science of Mastering Life's Greatest Challenges.* Cambridge, MA: Cambridge University Press, 2012.

Southwick, Steven M., Brett T. Litz, Dennis S. Charney, and Matthew J. Friedman, eds. *Resilience and Mental Health: Challenges across the Lifespan.* Cambridge, MA: Cambridge University Press, 2011.

Steele, Kathy, van der Hart, Onno, and Nijenhuis, Ellert R. "Phase-Oriented Treatment of Structural Dissociation in Complex Traumatization: Overcoming Trauma-Related Phobias." *Journal of Trauma Dissociation*, 6, no. 3 (2005):11–53. doi:10.1300/J229v06n03_02. PMID: 16172081.

Sternberg, Janine. *Infant Observation at the Heart of Training.* London: Routledge, 2018.

Sullivan, Harry Stack. *The Interpersonal Theory of Psychiatry.* New York: W. W. Norton, 1953.

Sullivan, Harry Stack. *The Psychiatric Interview.* New York: W. W. Norton, 1954.

Sullivan, Harry Stack. *Clinical Studies in Psychiatry.* New York: W. W. Norton, 1956.

Timerman, Jacobo. *Prisoner Without a Name, Cell Without a Number (Trans. Talbot, T.),* New York, 1981: Vintage, 1981.

Tronick, Edward Z. "Emotions and Communication in Infants." *American Psychologist* 44, no. 2 (1989): 112–119.

Tronick, Edward Z. *The Neurobehavioral and Social-Emotional Development of Infants and Children.* New York: W. W. Norton, 2007.

van der Kolk, Bessel. *The Body Keeps the Score: Brain, Mind, and Body in the Healing of Trauma.* New York: Penguin, 2014.

van Ijzendoorn, Marinus J., Carlo Schuengel, and Marian Bakermans-Kranenburg. "Disorganized Attachment in Early Childhood: Meta-Analysis of Precursors, Concomitants, and Sequelae." *Developmental Psychopathology* 11 no. 2 (1999): 225–249.

Vinkers, Christiaan H., Geuze, Elbert, van Rooij, Sanne J.H., Kennis, M., Schur, Remmelt R., Nispeling, Danny M., Smith, Alicia K., Nievergelt, Caroline L., Uddin, Monica, Rutten, Bart P. F., Vermetten, Eric, and Boks, Marco P. "Successful Treatment of Post-Traumatic Stress Disorder Reverses DNA Methylation Marks." *Molecular Psychiatry*, 2019. https://doi.org/10.1038/s41380-019-0549-3

Vonnegut, Kurt. *Breakfast of Champions.* New York: Delacorte Press, 1973.

Waring, E. M. and Chelune, Gordon J. "Marital Intimacy and Self-Disclosure." *Journal of Clinical Psychology* 39, no. 2 (1983). https://doi.org/10.1002/1097-4679(198303)39:2<183::AID-JCLP2270390206>3.0.CO;2-L

Winnicott, Donald W. *Playing and Reality.* London: Tavistock, 1971.

Yehuda, Rachel, Daskalakis, Nikolaos P., Desarnaud, Frank, Makotkine, Iouri, Lehrener, Amy, L., Koch, Erin, Flory, Janine D., Buxbaum, Joseph D., Meaney, Michael J., and Bierer, Linda M.. "Epigenetic Biomarkers as Predictors and Correlates of Symptom Improvement Following Psychotherapy in Combat Veterans with PTSD." *Psychiatry*, 27 September 2013. https://doi.org/10.3389/fpsyt.2013.00118

Žižek, Slavoj. *The Parallax View*. Cambridge, MA: MIT Press, 2006.

Žižek, Slavoj. *Violence: Six Sideways Reflections.* New York: Picador. 2008.

Žižek, Slavoj. *First as Tragedy, Then as Farce.* London: Verso, 2009.

ABOUT THE AUTHORS

Mark B. Borg, Jr., PhD, is a community and clinical psychologist and a psychoanalyst practicing in New York City. He is founding partner of The Community Consulting Group, a consulting firm that trains community stakeholders, local governments and other organizations to use psychoanalytic techniques in community rebuilding and revitalization. He is a supervisor of psychotherapy at the William Alanson White Institute and has written extensively about the intersection of psychoanalysis and community crisis intervention. He has published numerous articles and book chapters on community intervention, organizational consultation, psychoanalytic therapy; and on the application of psychoanalytic theory and technique to improve and streamline the process of community crisis intervention.

Grant H. Brenner, MD, FAPA, is a board-certified psychiatrist who brings nearly two decades of consultation, workshops, speaking engagements, therapy, and coaching to his clients, who range from individuals seeking to overcome emotional obstacles to leaders seeking to function better in the workplace. Dr. Brenner is a Fellow of both the American Psychiatric Association and the New York Academy of Medicine. He is on faculty at the Mount Sinai Beth Israel Hospital, former Director of Trauma Service at the William Alanson White Institute, and Co-Chair of Vibrant Emotional Health's Crisis and Emotional Care Team Advisory Board, Co-Chair of the Disasters, Trauma and Global Health Committee of the Group for Advancement of Psychiatry, and

CEO and co-founder of Neighborhood Psychiatry. With Dr. Fara White, Dr. Brenner co-hosts the *Doorknob Comments* podcast.

Daniel Berry, RN, MHA, has practiced as a registered nurse in New York City since 1987. Working in in-patient, home care, and community settings, his work has taken him into some of the city's most privileged households as well as some of its most underserved and dangerous public housing projects in Manhattan and the South Bronx. He is currently Assistant Director of Nursing for Risk Management at a public facility serving homeless and undocumented victims of street violence, addiction, and traumatic injuries. In 2015 he was invited to serve as a nurse consultant to a United Nations-certified NGO in Afghanistan that promotes community development and addresses women's and children's health issues.